MIDAS
MANAGERS

How Every Business They Touch Turns to Gold

Rob Slee

About the Author

Rob Slee is Managing Director of Robertson & Foley (www.robertsonfoley.com), a middle market investment banking firm.

Rob has published more than one hundred articles on private finance topics in a variety of legal and business journals. Rob's book, *Private Capital Markets*, was published in mid-2004 by John Wiley & Sons. This book is now considered the seminal work in finance for private companies.

Rob is a board member of numerous professional associations and private companies. He owns equity positions in a variety of mid-sized private businesses. He is a Phi Beta Kappa graduate of Miami University, and received a Master's degree from the University of Chicago and an MBA from Case Western Reserve University. Rob can be reached at: rob@robertsonfoley.com

Rob is best known as Jen and Jessie Slee's dad, his identical 17 year old twins.

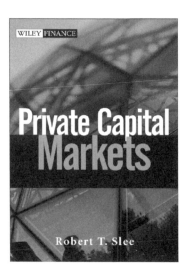

MIDAS MANAGERS

How Every Business They Touch Turns to Gold

Burn the Boats Press

Midas Managers
How Every Business They Touch Turns to Gold
www.midasmanagers.com

Edited by Andrew Park
Cover design and cartoons drawn by Greg Russell
Page design by Rosamond Grupp

Library of Congress Cataloging-in-Publication Data

Slee, Robert T.

  Midas Managers: how every business they touch turns to gold / Rob Slee – 1st ed.
    p.   cm.

    ISBN 978-0-9790478-1-7
    1. Private business-Strategy.   2. Success in business.   3. Global economy.
    I. Title

Contents

Part I – Introduction

Part II – Arbitrage

Part III – Business Models

Part IV – Private Finance

Part V – Conclusion

Part I

INTRODUCTION

Foreword

It seems the world is getting smaller every day. Technology, logistics and the Internet have combined to bring the planet to our doorstep. People from around the globe desperately want what we in the United States take for granted: two cars, a nice home, a good education for their kids, and enough food and money that these things are no longer a concern. Make no mistake, we're in the middle of the largest and most important economic war in humankind's history.

How do we win this war? The answer is somewhat surprising: we use our minds. There's no use competing solely with our backs; the Chinese, Indians and other less-developed countries far outnumber us. But we're armed with something no other population can match: a stubborn resilience to win no matter the odds.

The pages that follow show us how to prevail in this new Conceptual Age. Basically, we need to question and rethink everything. We need to slay the sacred cows and ignore the conventional wisdoms of the past. For instance, it's no longer enough to show up and do a good job – now we all need to add value, or we won't have a place at the economic table. Further, we each have an individual responsibility to amass the skills necessary to continue to add value. We can't rely on the government or companies to make this happen.

Having skills is only the ante in this new global game. We also need to employ strategic thinking, in ways that may seem foreign at first. For example, we all need to design value-added solutions for the stakeholders in our sphere of influence, then deliver the solutions in an effective manner. Most of what happens between design-and-delivery is outsourced. Imagine being able to triple your current output without adding any employees or requiring additional capital. That's the Midas way. And it's available to you - Now.

This is a fight we must win. Our financial independence is at stake. And that is something we can't take for granted.

Preface

Business has never been more competitive than in the 21st century. As we hear over and over, we now live in an always-on global economy powered by technology, logistics and the spread of capitalism to all corners of the world.

Today, large publicly held corporations are faring well because they buy and sell in global markets and have for years, but the same cannot be said for most private companies. They might buy globally, but they sell domestically. At best, America's privately owned businesses are getting only half the benefits of globalization.

"So what?" you might be asking yourself. Well, if our private companies aren't globally competitive, then they're in trouble. And if they're in trouble, we're all in trouble. Privately owned businesses generate more than 50 percent of America's gross domestic product and account for 80 percent of new jobs. On their own, U.S. private capital markets would rank as perhaps the world's largest economy. But we should be alarmed: Currently about 75% of owners of private businesses are not increasing the value of their firms. I'll say it again: If the private business sector fails, America fails.

Despite this, few of our leaders are doing anything to help. The federal government barely recognizes the existence of private markets, and few, if any, of its policies are designed with private business owners in mind. Apparently Washington is in business to serve Exxon and its intergalactic brethren. Here's a news flash: Exxon doesn't need our help. It and the other multinational behemoths on Wall Street can fend for themselves. It's Main Street that needs a helping hand right now. At the very least, politicians should stop talking about private companies as the engines of the U.S. economy and start doing something to get them firing on all cylinders.

Universities are also strangely silent when it comes to private business. Some have started entrepreneurial centers, often funded by alumni who made their fortunes in the private capital markets, and that's a good start. However, academics have historically looked down on small business and the majority still teach as if running IBM is their students' likely career path. And don't even get me started on MBA programs. Public companies reign supreme there. As one Dean of a business school told me: "If only we had more data and information on private markets, we would be more inclined to teach something about them." Excuse me, but I thought that's what academics did – study and organize bodies of knowledge.

Even business books aren't helping owners and managers of private firms compete better. While I enjoy vague references to possible solutions as much as the next person, running a business successfully requires something more detailed, like a blueprint for major investments. Most business books examine a few large public companies and then attempt to distill lofty truisms for the masses to follow. Little of this Welchian dogma applies to private companies or teaches their owners and managers how to make wealth-creating decisions.

I have felt a salmon-like urge to write this book. For the last 20 years, I have provided investment banking services to literally thousands of privately owned businesses. Two years ago I authored a textbook, *Private Capital Markets*, which was the first work to explore and describe the field of private finance in an integrated and comprehensive way. This new field does not rely on corporate finance theories, which describe behavior in public capital markets; it uses constructs that explain, organize, and predict behavior in private markets.

Understanding and using private capital markets theory gives companies an advantage over their competitors, and *Private Capital Markets* is a great place for students to learn it. Most owners and managers, however, don't have the time to pick up a textbook. They need a practical guide that will help them run private businesses in this era of hyper-competition. *Midas Managers* is just that book. It raises the ante, challenging readers to rethink everything they know about business and learn how to create wealth in an always-on, global economy.

The backdrop of *Midas Managers* is that the world has entered a new Age of business called the Conceptual Age. With each new Age, the rules of doing business have changed – and the Conceptual Age is no different. Of course, no one needs to tell owners and managers that things are different. They're just not sure what to do about it.

This book fills in the blanks. In it, I tell 18.5 stories of how private business owners and managers developed innovative strategies to create value for their companies and wealth for themselves. I was involved in nearly all of these situations as an investment banker, and I call these men and women Midas Managers, because they truly have a golden touch. Each of their stories is followed by a "Blueprint," which provides step-by-step instructions for readers who want to employ these strategies in their own businesses.

Note that I am not attempting to convert ordinary businesspeople into Midas Managers. Reading a book isn't going to do that for anyone. It usually takes a cataclysmic life-changing event to cause a Midas transformation. However, I do believe owners and managers can use Midas strategies to create wealth in their own companies. By definition, it takes a Midas Manager to create a Midas strategy, but anyone can replicate that strategy.

Also, be aware that in these pages I am using *value* and *wealth* interchangeably. In actuality, value is unrealized wealth. In other words, value is built in the business and wealth is then realized through some liquidity event, such as the sale of the business.

Midas Managers is organized into three sections, one for each of the three types of Midas strategies I describe: Arbitrage, Business Models, and Private Finance. Each section contains a brief introduction, followed by a handful of story chapters. Other than Ken Iverson and Nucor Steel in Chapter 25, the names, companies, and details of each story have been changed to protect the privacy of the individuals involved.

A number of cartoons appear throughout the book. The hero, "Investment Banker Man," was dreamed up by my twins when they were six and — like the rest of my family — having trouble understanding what Daddy did for a living. One day, they saw me transform my attire from bum to investment banker, then back again. Later someone asked them what their father did for a living. "He's Investment Banker Man!" they replied with pride.

I wish to thank the thousands of people who contributed to this book. From the beginning it has been a group effort. In fact, there are too many of you to name individually. You know who you are and that I will be forever grateful.

Goals of this Book

I have several goals for this book:

1. To create an awareness that globalization has dramatically changed the ways business wealth is created, especially for small and mid-sized private companies;

2. To offer a framework in which creating wealth from a private business in this new Age can be organized, explained, and predicted;

3. To describe and analyze strategies that Midas Managers have used to create wealth in their businesses;

4. To outline how any owner or manager can implement a Midas strategy in his or her company.

Of course, most private business owners and managers will need some outside help. They don't spend large parts of their day considering financial strategies, nor do most small to mid-sized private companies have folks dedicated to this task. However, this book gives them a unique opportunity to plan how they're going to create wealth. Their lawyers, investment bankers, CPAs, M&A intermediaries, estate planners, and other advisers can then assist them with implementing that plan. And if they can't, they should be replaced immediately.

Finally, as I wrote this book, I was struck by how much has changed in just a short period of time. The world has flattened out, change is happening at ever-increasing rates, and each of us has a responsibility to compete and add value, no matter who we are. That imperative reminds me what legendary golfer and Midas Manager Bobby Jones once said: "Competitive golf is played mainly on a five-inch course – the space between your ears." This book is dedicated to everyone competing in the new Age, which requires mastery of precisely the same field of play.

INVESTMENT BANKER MAN

Translation: Record sales for the Italian designers,
Indian engineers, and Chinese manufacturers

Midas Managers

Some businesspeople intuitively know how to create wealth. They are constantly increasing the value of their business holdings, regardless of industry conditions or economic cycles. It's more than good luck, since the same people strike gold again and again. These wealth-creators just seem to have the Midas touch. I call them Midas Managers.

Midas Managers are a rare breed: they account for less than 1% of all businesspeople. This, in part, explains the lack of value currently being created by private owners. Less than a quarter of private companies in the U.S. will be worth more in five years than they are today.

Midas Managers are also unusual people. They build substantial wealth based on market knowledge, and the ability, as legendary entrepreneur Ted Turner describes it, to see "just over the horizon." They are motivated by money, but seek to create both personal and business wealth. They focus on a few critical success factors and use straightforward metrics to measure their progress toward them. They understand the behavior and motives of players around them. They are reflective, but with enough salesmanship to get what they want. They think strategically, but act practically. They usually master only one or two wealth-creating strategies; then they look for situations where they can apply these same strategies over and over. More often than not, they are contrarians. J. Paul Getty, a Midas Manager of the first degree, famously summed up their mindset when he said that "no one can possibly achieve any real and lasting success ... by being a conformist."

Of course, Midas Managers have existed as long as there's been commercial activity. Their names are very familiar to any student of business: Medici, Rothschild, Morgan, Rockefeller, Buffett, and Gates. Most Midas Managers, however, do not have familiar names. Only their families and community know that they "fell into something." It is this lesser-known group that interests me, especially their ability to create wealth from relatively small companies even during changing times. This book contains their stories.

New Rules of Wealth Creation

Every so often the rules of business change. In the past 200 years this has occurred several times. First came the Industrial Revolution, which in the early 19th century ushered in the Industrial Age. John Henry may have beaten the mechanical spike-driver in lore, but machines have dominated in every other way for more than 150 years. Next came the Information Age, which began in the 1950's with the arrival of computers and reached a climax in the 1990's with the explosion of the Internet. Computers changed the way we work, making complex jobs easy and enabling routine tasks to be performed at ever-lower costs. During this Age, knowledge workers and MBAs reigned supreme.

Now we have entered the Conceptual Age. On September 11, 2001, the United States was thrust into a global war with terrorists. At about the same time, China entered the World Trade Organization. The combination of these events birthed the Conceptual Age and thrust U.S. businesses into a global war of their own. The Conceptual Age marks the intersection of globalization, logistics, and advanced technology. This Age is defined by multi-dimensional thinking. This Age requires business owners to conceptualize their way to success. Operational excellence is no longer enough. In the Conceptual Age, it is merely the starting point. Machines, capital and employees are no longer the main factors in creating business wealth. In the Conceptual Age, the biggest is the manager's ability to conceptualize solutions. Walt Disney would be proud: our imaginations are now the major constraint on wealth creation.

There are various ways to describe behavior required for creating wealth in the Conceptual Age. But the most important skills center on the human mind, or, more precisely, on the two hemispheres of the brain. The Information Age worked the left side of our brains, where we do heavy analytical lifting; success in the current Age relies on the right side, the source of our creativity. In his book, *A Whole New Mind: Moving from the Information Age to the Conceptual Age*, author Daniel H. Pink argues that the left brain capabilities that ruled the Information Age, while still necessary, aren't sufficient in the Conceptual Age. The skill sets required now reflect the imperative placed on design, innovation and market knowledge in the 21st century. As children, many of us were told to avoid artistic careers in favor of a more reliable future in business. In the Conceptual Age, our ability to be "artsy" will in large part determine our success in business. In a world where the major resources are available to everyone, it is the ability to do more with less that separates winners from losers.

Companies today compete in a technology-enabled, logistics-powered, globalized economy. Competition is no longer local, it's global, and the rules of wealth creation have changed. Let's consider some of the New Rules:

1. Every person working in or for a business must create value to remain employed.
2. Job security is a function of the number of value-creating skill sets a person possesses.

3. A company can expand its returns through arbitrage if its managers understand how to exploit market opportunities.

4. Companies should adopt conceptual business models to create wealth. As such, a company should control – not own – its process chain.

5. In order to make good investment and financing decisions, and thereby create wealth, managers must raise their Private Finance I.Q.

Although playing by these New Rules will help business owners and managers create wealth, we can't escape the paradoxical nature of the Conceptual Age. This is best illustrated by the first entry in the "rules to consider" section of Wikipedia, the volunteer- written Internet encyclopedia: Ignore all rules.

Skill Sets and Value

The notion that everyone is responsible for his or her own value creation is a new one. Until recently, most people have assumed that doing a good job was enough. Training, development, and even education were shared responsibilities: employers and the government were charged with ensuring everyone's personal competitiveness. This changed in the 1980s when corporations began downsizing, thus breaking the Employer-Employee contract. Since then, whether they know it or not, everybody has been responsible for developing and maintaining value-creating skill sets.

A skill set consists of the capabilities needed to complete a major task. The Three R's - reading, 'riting and 'rithmetic - are not skill sets. The ability to use chemistry to create new formulas is a skill set. The ability to write legal contracts is a skill set. Yet with the exception of technical and engineering programs, most schools do not teach skill sets; rather, students are taught how to learn skill sets.

In a globalized world, job security is directly related to the number and quality of value-creating skill sets a person possesses. Of course, possessing a skill set does not guarantee value creation, because demand patterns change. For instance, unless she updated her skills, the best DOS-era programmer probably no longer creates value. Everyone needs to constantly update and add to his or her skills to continue to create value. And one skill set is not enough. Several inter-connected, value-creating skill sets are needed to ensure personal competitiveness. An ancillary benefit of acquiring skill sets is that it inevitably leads to the development of a more sophisticated view of the market place and what's required to win.

Arbitrage

It's human nature to want something for nothing. This feeling is enhanced when what's offered for free is worth millions of dollars. Arbitrage business strategies convert this feeling into reality. The word smells of money and it's frequently used in the same breath with words like "fortune," "boatload" or "killing." The dictionary defines arbitrage as the simultaneous purchase and sale of the same securities in different markets to profit from unequal prices. I define arbitrage as the ability to create wealth by taking advantage of inter-market opportunities. Managers create an arbitraged return when they understand capital markets well enough to discover and exploit a risk/return imbalance in the market. Properly implemented, arbitrage strategies enable a manager to receive a return that is greater than the underlying risk of the investment.

Arbitrage opportunities present themselves to managers who understand that capital markets are segmented. Capital markets are segmented based on a number of factors. The two most obvious are annual revenues and the return expectations of investors. The following Exhibit depicts this segmentation. The broadest market segments include the small business market, the middle market and the large company market. Within the middle market, further segmentation is possible into lower-, middle- and upper-middle markets. Each market is subject to different return expectations, as demonstrated by acquisition multiples based on earnings before interest, taxes, depreciation and amortization (EBITDA). Small companies typically sell for two to three times EBITDA, while large companies sell for more than 12 times EBITDA. Exploiting the market's notion that "bigger is better" can create substantial value for a business owner.

Market Segmentation by Sales and EBITDA Acquisition Multiples

Sales ($millions)	5		150		500		1,000	
Small Businesses		Lower		Middle		Upper		Large Companies
		M i d d l e			M a r k e t			
EBITDA	2-3x	4-7x		8-9x		10-12x		>12x

Suppose a manager wants to realize a higher selling multiple for his company. One arbitrage strategy involves the manager consolidating his or her way there by paying acquisition multiples that are less than what the market would pay for his or her company. Thus, a manager of a middle-middle market company could acquire lower-middle market companies in order to eventually realize an exit in the upper-middle market. This creates an arbitraged return. In the vernacular of public companies, such a strategy would be accretive to shareholders. Not surprisingly, most arbitrage strategies depend on effective use of know-how, also known as intellectual capital.

Conceptual Business Models

Business models — the ways a company plans, organizes, and controls to meet its goals — have also changed in the Conceptual Age. Old-style "traditional" business models destroy wealth if they do not respect the New Rules. Conceptual business models, by contrast, are based on the New Rules. Consider Cirque du Soleil, or Dell, or Southwest Airlines. All three companies reconceptualized prevailing business models and in so doing both revolutionized their industries and created substantial value for their owners.

In these changing times, managers have no choice but to adopt conceptual business models to create wealth. Conceptual business models organize a company's process chain around the realities of globalization and the opportunities afforded by logistics and advanced technology. Simply put, a process chain is the set of activities a firm must undertake to supply its product or service. For example, in a traditional wood-processing domestic process chain timber is harvested by American loggers; American logs are sawed, then kiln-dried; dried boards are then shipped or further processed. This process chain worked well for more than a century. Then, in the 1980's, other countries began shipping finished boards into the U.S., sometimes at a fraction of the American producers' cost. Almost overnight the process chain in the forest products industry changed. Yet, many American owners were so accustomed to the old ways of doing business that they refused to change. Even after they went bankrupt, these owners did not understand the New Rules.

What did Midas Managers in the forest products industry do? They compared their internal costs at each step of their process chain with the new entrants' pricing, and then made a "build versus buy" calculation. At each step where their company could no longer create value for itself, Midas Managers purchased the good from, or outsourced the service to, another company.

In most cases this involved shuttering sawmills and other operations, something an ordinary manager would not do because it would have meant forgoing revenue and shrinking the company. The Midas Manager recognized that reducing the overall sales of his or her company actually increased profitability dramatically.

Control – Don't Own – Your Process Chain

Thanks to globalization, for the first time in mankind's history, everyone on the planet has access to all of the world's natural resources. Europeans, Asians, and Americans can all access Brazilian rainforests, Chinese factories, and rooms full of Indian technologists. What separates the winners if everyone has access to the same resources and thus, the same cost structure? The ability to harness, develop and implement intellectual capital. In other words, whoever creates the most value from the communal resources wins. This is the province of Midas Managers.

An example will illustrate this point. Let's assume that companies in Europe, Japan, and the United States each spot a market opportunity at the same time: a new type of lean-back chair. This potential niche is identified in an article in a leading medical journal that shows a person watching television will suffer less back pain and fatigue if they are sitting in a chair that tilts backwards at exactly 120 degrees. But no such chair is available in the market. All three companies have access to the same materials and cost structure to assemble such a chair. Who will dominate the market? The answer: whichever company creates the most value to the customer.

The Midas approach is to own the intellectual capital but not the entire process chain. For instance, design of the chair is a critical success factor. That intellectual capital must be owned by the company. But all of the manufacturing can be outsourced. All of the distribution can be outsourced. Even marketing of the chair can be controlled but not owned. The Midas Manager knows that the winning company has a rapid response to the market, at a low cost, but a high value to the consumer.

Conceptual business models can also take advantage of what the market will give you. This is a niche-based approach. A niche not only represents an unmet customer need, it is also a sustainable intra-market business opportunity to create wealth. Niches often appear out of the corner of a business owner's eye. Many Midas Managers have told me that their best niches sprung from off-hand comments made by customers. One manager of an industrial distribution company once heard a contractor mention that it would be great if the distributor could create and supply stock lists from job blueprints. The Midas Manager immediately recognized that this service could create a competitive advantage and would allow him to position his company in a new, lucrative and sustainable niche.

Midas Managers are niche-aholics. To create wealth, business owners should be thinking in niches, too. This is true for several reasons. First, niches are identified through insightful process chain management. Activities such as outsourcing and intellectual capital development reinforce a company's ability to find and take advantage of niches. Second, capital and other resources are highly constrained for most private companies; this prohibits these companies from being all things to all customers. Third, niche-based strategies help private managers align their companies with one of the main realities of globalization: ever-increasing competition.

Over the past twenty years, globalization has caused the average niche size to drop substantially. This is because companies from around the world are now competing for every piece of business, no matter how small. A combination of more sophisticated logistics and the Internet opening up information flows has created niches with less than $5 million in annual sales. Many wealth-creating middle market companies are in fact just amalgams of fairly small niche businesses.

Private Finance IQ

Where does someone learn the New Rules of the Conceptual Age? The intellectual skill sets needed to create wealth are not learned in school. Even our greatest universities have not stepped up to the challenge of teaching the development and implementation of intellectual capital. This is why Midas Managers have had to learn these skill sets in the school of hard knocks. One Midas Manager explained it this way: "The most important learning happens when I get out my checkbook." In other words, you pay for your education whether you're in school or not.

Even with a conceptual business model, however, most managers need to raise their Private Finance IQ's to create wealth. Private Finance is the discipline that helps managers of private companies create wealth by making better investment and financing decisions. The typical manager's Private Finance I.Q. is low. For example, most managers do not know their company's cost of capital, nor do they know why it's vitally important to know it. Capital has a cost and this cost is measured on an "all-in" basis, not just stated interest rates. Moreover, corporate wealth is not created until a company achieves returns greater than its cost of capital. "Until a business returns a profit that is greater than its cost of capital, it operates at a loss," management guru Peter Drucker told *Fortune* magazine in 1998. "Never mind that it pays taxes as if it had a genuine profit. The enterprise still returns less to the economy than it devours in resources. Until then it does not create wealth; it destroys it."

As Chapter 4 illustrates, finance for private companies is quite different from finance for public firms. For example, the typical private company possesses a cost of capital that is nearly twice as high as a large public company. Thus, private firms can not create wealth simply by slugging it out against their larger competitors. But private owners who adopt strategies that either increase returns or reduce their cost of capital have an advantage over owners with a lower Private Finance I.Q.

In Search of the Midas Touch

I'm often asked, "Can anyone become a Midas Manager?" The answer, I'm sorry to say, is "no." While the strategies herein can be replicated and implemented by any manager in any industry, no book is going to give that manager the Midas touch. Midas Managers are born on life's battlefield, often via some cataclysmic event that occurs early in life. For example, many famous Midas Managers were breadwinners for their families before they turned 13. The rest of us must be content to look over their shoulders and learn their tricks. When it comes to Midas Managers, imitation is not only the sincerest form of flattery, it might also lead to substantial wealth creation.

INVESTMENT BANKER MAN

The secret chant of raising venture capital

Essence of Midas

It's difficult to definitively describe Midas Managers. They come in all shapes and sizes. They aren't created in classrooms or training programs. They do not announce themselves when they enter a room. In most cases, they don't flaunt the substantial wealth they've earned. Yet they exist.

A caveat: I do not believe this book, or any other for that matter, can increase the number of Midas Managers in the world. Less than 1 percent of managers throughout history have had these unique abilities. This is not surprising, since most occurrences in nature can be described via a normal distribution. Warren Buffett, the quintessential modern-day Midas Manager, has often been labeled a Six Sigma, a reference to his position to the extreme right of the mean of all investors. Still, all managers can benefit by implementing Midas strategies. Perhaps this is an extension of the Dilbert Principle, which says that only a handful of enlightened individuals live in each generation. These enlightened ones enable the rest of us to enjoy plasma-screen TVs and iPODs. If Midas Managers are the guiding lights that enable others to create value, so be it.

Even though we can't create Midas Managers, we need to understand their essence. This is true for several reasons. First, some people possess Midas attributes, but aren't working in the business world. Perhaps some of these Midas Managers-to-be can be encouraged to take the leap. Second, before copying someone, it's nice to know how they tick. It's not all blocking and tackling out there. A good bit of the game of business is knowing when to dodge or duck. Midas Managers understand the role of nuance in business success.

Nearly all Midas Managers were thrown into challenging circumstances at too young an age. In the case of John D. Rockefeller, he was literally thrown into a pond, as this was the standard teaching technique employed by his father. Other Midas Managers were the breadwinners for their family before they reached 13, including Andrew Carnegie. At the very least, some major event occurred that shaped the rest of their Midas lives. For Ken Iverson, founder of Midas-managed company Nucor Steel, this make-or-break event occurred when he was 16: He wrecked his dad's new car. Upon hearing the news, his father asked whether anyone was injured. When Ken said "no," his father directed him to fix the car himself. Ken protested that he didn't know how to repair a totaled car, which, of course, played right into his father's plan. For the next year Ken worked on every part of the vehicle until it was like brand new. Ken later said that after this episode he never feared anything again.

There are a handful of traits that most Midas Managers have in common, as follows:

- They intuitively sense opportunities to create value
- They can see over the horizon
- They understand that hard work is not enough
- They understand the motives of others
- They boil projects down to a few critical success factors
- They tend to be contrarians
- They are control freaks in pursuit of a goal

Midas Managers have an innate ability to spot a value-creating opportunity, and they don't fall victim to paralysis-by-analysis. It took Howard Hughes less than five minutes to decide to place the two biggest bets of his life: producing the most expensive movie ever made and acquiring Trans World Airlines. When asked why, in both cases Hughes answered, "I just know it will work." While most Midas Managers consider make-or-break investments more carefully than that, they all arrive at their decisions in the same intuitive way: They just know it will work.

Midas Managers have the ability to see how a game is going to end before the cards have been played. I heard Ted Turner explain it as being able to see "just over the horizon." My great aunt, a highly successful business owner and Midas Manager herself, likened it to telling a story. She said that business success happens when you can describe how the story will end before it begins.

They're not slackers, but Midas Managers understand that there is an inverse relationship between hours worked and success. In the early years they might burn the midnight oil, but few Midas Managers work long weeks as a matter of course. Since they understand the motives of others, Midas Managers are able to use those around them to do the work. Partly this is a matter of delegation; partly it is a matter of understanding what their stakeholders require and then providing it. According to Ron Chernow, in *Titan: The Life of John D. Rockefeller, Sr.,* at Standard Oil, John D. Rockefeller required every manager to train a subordinate to do his job. As Rockefeller explained, "Nobody does anything if he can get anybody else to do it ... as soon as you can, get someone whom you can rely on, train him in the work, sit down, cock up your heels, and think out some way for the Standard Oil Company to make some money."

Midas Managers distill business "noise" into a handful of critical success factors. Then they ferociously manage these factors. By following just a few financial metrics, they can keep a finger on the pulse of the business. As one Midas Manager in North Carolina explained it, "If I know our order book, gross margin, and cash position, I know if we're winning." As Warren Buffett says, "We like simple businesses."

Midas Managers are almost always contrarians. It's a natural instinct for Midas Managers to swim against the current. To use a different metaphor from nature, they understand that if you follow the pack, you get pack returns. Andrew Carnegie attributed his enormous success to simply knowing when to buy and sell: the time to buy was when everyone was selling and vice versa. In his biography of Buffett, Andrew Kilpatrick explained why the great investor's famous individualism was so special: "Our day-to-day lives don't prepare us in the least for going against the crowd. In almost everything we do, success is a function of how well we go along with the crowd, not how well we go against it. As a result, going against the crowd, and ignoring what psychologists call social proof, is contrary to our nature. Little wonder value investing is so tough, and so little used. Most people don't have the psychological musculature to carry the burden of negative opinion that goes with fifty-cent dollars."

Midas Managers tend to employ only one or two value-creating strategies that work for them over and again. This explains why Midas Managers can parachute into any industry and create value. They only get involved in a situation when they believe their strategies will work. Ken Iverson developed one primary strategy for Nucor: He got workers to identify their interests with those of the company, something managers have been attempting, with little success, since the dawn of industry. Iverson did it at Nucor; he could have done it in any industry.

Midas Managers tend to be control freaks. Their single-minded obsession with achieving their goals is what drives them to excel. While those around them would like to succeed, Midas Managers use force of will to make certain it happens. They are out to prove something to somebody. Occasionally they just want to prove it to their own satisfaction. Most of the time, though, there is an external force driving them, maybe a former employer, a disbelieving spouse or doubting relatives.

Midas Managers are not universally successful. Indeed, they have a special relationship with failure: they learn from their mistakes and win the big bets. This connection is summed up nicely by this Chinese proverb: "Rare is the successful person who hasn't been fired or bankrupt **at least once**."

Midas Managers take persistence to a whole new level. This passage from Calvin Coolidge could be the Midas Manager Credo:

> *Press on. Nothing in the world can take the place of persistence.*
> *Talent will not: Nothing is more common than unsuccessful*
>   *individuals with talent.*
> *Genius will not: Unrewarded genius is almost a proverb.*
> *Education will not: The world is full of educated derelicts.*
> *Persistence, along with patience and prudence, determines*
>   *business success.*

Midas Managers are unusually persistent toward achieving a single goal, but unlike entrepreneurs, who are risk takers, Midas Managers are risk avoiders. Once again, Kilpatrick writes that Warren Buffett made this point when he said that the "secret to making money is not to take risks, but to avoid them. We've done better by avoiding dragons rather than by slaying them." Ted Turner has said he was never a reckless gambler, even though his rakish image might have led some to think otherwise.

Most Midas Managers are "impatiently patient." They expect that it will take as long as it takes to meet a goal, but they also believe progress requires constant goading. They don't call it quits even when conventional wisdom might encourage them otherwise. They're content to realize their goals year by year, day by day, step by step, and inch by inch. And Midas Managers can stomach the inevitable rough patches along the way. When these managers are asked why they didn't give in, the answer is always the same: There's no difference between the struggle and their existence. If they lose the will to fight, they lose their very essence, and this tension never wanes.

Finally, Midas Managers are prudent. They follow the "First Penny" rule: the first penny from any business dealing stays in the business. Let others earn their own pennies. In fact, Penny Pinchers might be another appropriate moniker for this group. Midas Managers understand that it's easier and less risky to make money by controlling costs than by investing and earning. They undertake the latter only when the odds are heavily in their favor.

Saints Need Not Apply

Most Midas Managers are not saints. Many aren't even thought to be well-adjusted. Ted Turner was an apparent philanderer and narcissist whose erratic behavior in the workplace bordered on neurotic. But the man sure created a lot of wealth. Bill Gates' paranoia is legendary. He's still driven by a fear that someone is coming to get him, and with all of those billions in the bank, he's probably right. Howard Hughes? His unorthodox behavior put him in a class by himself, but so did his enormous success in business. Despite this, Midas Managers are often self-righteous in their dealings. Once again, Rockefeller provides an example. His finest qualities as a businessman were often on display right alongside his most craven: visionary leadership, courageous persistence, a capacity to think in strategic terms, but also a lust for domination, a messianic certitude, and contempt for those short-sighted mortals who made the mistake of standing in his way. Chernow writes that Rockefeller's view of money was "what's mine is mine, and what's yours is mine." How he got "yours" was more a matter of details than conscience.

Yes, the will-to-win is extremely strong in Midas Managers. They use whatever means are necessary to get the job done. Andrew Carnegie formed and broke alliances at the drop of a hat to further his goals. Cosimo Medici, patriarch of the famous Italian family, employed a combination of political savvy and piles of money to assure success – without much concern for Florentine law (it says a lot about Cosimo's methods that Machiavelli identified him as one of his chief role models).

In the end, money is the ultimate scorecard for Midas Managers. They are highly motivated to earn it, and the desire to accumulate vast sums of it is a constant refrain. Says Bill Gates, in Janet Lowe's *Bill Gates Speaks*: "Business is a good game: lots of competition and a minimum of rules. You keep score with money." According to Kilpatrick, even Warren Buffett, who is famous for being frugal, believes "there are more important things than money, and one of them is a lot of money." And when Andrew Carnegie was 25 years old, and not yet wealthy, he declared his intention to be the richest man in the world.

The Good News

Midas Managers exist in all walks of life. The traits listed above can be found in high school principals, police sergeants, emergency room nurses, basketball coaches, and many other professionals. Although this book describes value creation in a business setting, many of the same Midas Managers herein went on to create substantial social value in more altruistic settings using the very same strategies. Indeed, many Midas Managers ultimately tire of making money and shift their focus to giving it away. Andrew Carnegie, who spent the last years of his life giving away his vast fortune, almost single-handedly established the concept of public libraries around the world. Ted Turner is in the process of giving more than $1 billion to the United Nations. Bill Gates and Warren Buffett have already donated billions to improve health care and education through Gates' foundation. For all their quirkiness, obsessiveness and erratic behavior, Midas Managers have perfected strategies that have been responsible for some of our greatest achievements, whether they created wealth or just bettered society. Copied correctly, they can help the rest of us achieve a little greatness of our own.

3

Checkers or Chess?

Rockefeller called business a game: whoever knows the rules and plays by them most skillfully wins. Well, the game has changed. Think about it this way: in the Information Age, business managers were playing checkers; in the Conceptual Age, they have to play chess. Online. Against the world.

Checkers and chess can be played on the same board, but the games could not be more different. Checkers is a fairly simple game. The only moves are diagonal and forward. Chess, by comparison, is full of complexities: pieces move in multiple ways. Checkers is a tactical game. Every move after the first one is reactive and one-dimensional. Chess moves, on the other hand, require both tactical and strategic thinking. The game demands collaboration between pieces and a skilled player thinks five to seven moves ahead. Checkers, in other words, is a left brain game; chess uses both hemispheres.

Of course, all games have one thing in common: you can't play without first learning the rules. I've laid out some of the New Rules for creating value in the Conceptual Age. Left brain players aren't comfortable with the New Rules, but right brain players love them. Under the New Rules, operational effectiveness is a given and strategic thinking is what sets businesses apart. This is a bad news/good news situation. The bad news is that managers have not been trained to think strategically. In school, they were taught discrete subjects (English is Period 1; Math in Period 2, and so on), and most of their on-the-job training was tactical (how to drive a truck, lay a brick, assemble a car, etc.). Few people learn to sew these pieces into a strategic quilt. The good news is that Midas Managers have developed strategies that create wealth under the New Rules; strategies that anyone can imitate.

The Strategy Thing

It's interesting to note that when asked what role in a chess game they would choose to emulate, most business owners say the King or Queen, rather than the correct answer: the Player. The Player, after all, is the only one who knows the rules. The Player is the only one capable of seeing the entire board. The Player is the only one capable of having a strategy.

Only a small percentage of managers know how to play chess or how to think about business strategically. In other words, most business owners are vision-rich, but strategy-poor. They go into business with a mission but were never educated on the best ways to accomplish it. Strategy, as corporate strategy guru Michael Porter says, is a race to an ideal position. Every player hopes to do well in this race – but hope is not an effective strategy. Sound strategies enable managers to win the race, to make their vision reality.

Most private business owners are not strategic about their business, they are tactical. Tactics are not strategies; tactics are actions that support strategies. Tactics are the operating decisions that move the ball up the field. Think of the difference between tactics and strategy this way: majors and captains decide which tactics will win the battle; presidents and generals devise the strategies to win the war. Today, most business owners are playing the part of a major when they should be thinking like a Commander-in-Chief.

Midas Managers know the only way to create wealth from a private business is to employ strategies that will achieve at least one of three objectives: increase return, decrease risk, or improve the company's market position.

Why is strategy so important? Because creating wealth is a choice. It is not predestined that some people become wealthy while others do not. We all make choices throughout our lives that determine where we'll end up on the wealth curve. And even those who choose to be wealthy will face a never-ending series of walls along the path to increasing the value of their businesses. Getting over them requires strategy.

Never-ending Walls

What's the major constraint on creating value that every business faces? Is it the lack of market opportunities, the inability to attract the right employees, or the failure to raise capital? While these are undeniable challenges, the number one constraint every business faces is whoever is sitting at the owner's desk! Every owner must determine the strategies that will get the company over the next wall in its way. And while this has never been easy, the New Rules have made it even tougher.

Walls are metaphors for market, organizational, capital, and revenue obstacles that every firm faces as it tries to create wealth. Market walls represent the constantly changing demands that customers impose on companies, making it harder for them to grow sales, profitability, or value. In any Age, the process of understanding and meeting customer needs, a company's value proposition, is the first key to creating wealth. But the Conceptual Age has added some height to market walls. For example, worldwide competition has made establishing a profitable supply chain more difficult than ever. And with change occurring geometrically, it is harder than ever for managers to stay in front of trends shaping their industries.

Tom Rudolph, the Midas Manager whose story is told in Chapter 10, faces a market wall: his company must get bigger to create value. Changing customer requirements in his industry are making smaller companies uncompetitive. In fact, in any industry, most companies doing less than $5 million in annual revenues are not creating value. So Tom *consolidates* his way over the market wall. In just a few years, he creates a company ringing up more than $150 million in sales, and in so doing, generates wealth of more than $100 million. For him, the grass is greener on the other side of the wall.

Even though operating excellence is the starting point in the current Age, every company must overcome organizational walls, too. The foundation for the organizational wall is the owner's personal motivation. If an owner is not motivated to create value, she won't. Only the other guy hits the lottery or gets lucky in business. The rest of us must strive for success and work tirelessly to achieve it. And even a motivated owner needs a conceptual business model, which, when properly constructed, enables the company to maximize its resources under the New Rules. Unlike traditional business models, conceptual business models must be supported by human and intellectual capital.

Scott Livingston, the subject of Chapter 13, leverages his organization to create a "design and deliver" conceptual business model. By designing value-added solutions, outsourcing manufacturing, and then delivering the final products to his customers, Scott was able to generate tremendous productivity — sales of $2.5 million and profits of more than $500,000 – per employee!

Capital represents another wall in the way of creating value. Most owners believe financial capital is their biggest constraint. Without money, they can't grow, they surmise. But their cost of capital, not the sheer amount, actually determines the height of the wall. And the more challenging limitation in the Conceptual Age is the creation, development, and implementation of intellectual capital, a fancy term for brain power. Converting intellectual capital into cash has become a top-three job for managers.

Jen Taylor, the Midas Manager in Chapter 21, has capital. But she wants to know if her capital decisions are adding value to her business, and if so, how much. Not able to find a method that fit her circumstances, she created her own. Knowing how to calculate economic value in her company helped her make better decisions about investing capital and ultimately generate more wealth.

A company's size can act as a wall, too. The first big wall to scale in one industry might be $1 million in annual sales. The next major wall in that industry might be $4 to $5 million, then $10 to $12 million, then $25 million, and so on. There are a handful of ways that a manager can move his company to the other side of a revenue wall. He can:

- Use a ladder and scale the wall. Watch out for hot oil!
- Blow through the wall. It works in the movies but is more likely to blow up the company.
- Jump over the wall, like a pole vaulter. The mental image here is not positive.
- Get pulled over the wall by a customer – kicking, screaming and cussing.
- Think his way over the wall. Not even Rodin's *Thinker* would have conceived this.

Overcoming walls in the Conceptual Age requires adopting a new set of "ing" words: designing; conceiving; planning; strategizing, collaborating. In most cases, the business model must change to get over a wall. Roles of key managers must change, too. Owners of companies with $4 to $5 million in annual sales typically have the following characteristics: they wear 4-5 hats (or more); their management style is to react to things happening within the company; they use some information to make important decisions; they have little visibility into the business due to inadequate systems; they have a management team of one or two people. Now let's compare what owners of a businesses with $10 to $12 million in annual sales look like: they wear only a few hats; they manage through proactive planning; they use information to make key decisions; they have visibility into their business; they have built a management team with three to four key players. See how the roles of managers must shift from one sales level to the next?

The inability or unwillingness to reconceptualize is the main reason managers fail to climb the next wall no matter what kind of wall it is. But there's good news: Midas strategies can help.

Back to the Game

To understand how new rules have changed the game, consider the following challenge I give to firms that I influence:

In the next 3 years let's at least double sales, raise profits no less than ten-fold – and do this with half as many employees as we have today!

The first thought most managers would have is these things can't be done. And that's true under a traditional business model. In the Conceptual Age, though, achieving goals like these is not only possible. For those who want to compete globally and create wealth for their companies, it's mandatory.

The game of business has changed. New skills, paradigms, and mindsets are required to succeed in the Conceptual Age. Players must think conceptually and plan strategically to scale walls that stand in the way of value creation. Tactics alone aren't enough. Get ready for a wicked game of chess.

INVESTMENT BANKER MAN

But this is a game with which I'm not familiar

4

What You Need to Know About Finance

As a starting point for this discussion, forget everything you've ever been taught about finance. Chances are you don't remember much anyway. Over the past 30 years, millions of students around the world have been taught corporate finance principles. But virtually none of what's been taught can help you make good investment and financing decisions for a private business.

How is it possible that so little relevant information has been imparted? Because corporate finance is concerned almost exclusively with the financial behavior of large public companies. Yet, out of 10 million companies in the U.S., only 14,000 are publicly held, and only 2,000 of these are considered "large." The rest, for the most part, are small, privately owned businesses.

The top-selling finance textbook, *Principles of Corporate Finance,* by Richard A. Brealey and Stewart C. Myers, is typical in its neglect of private companies. Only one passage in the 1,100 page book even acknowledges them: "When a corporation is first established, its shares may all be held by a small group of investors, perhaps the company's managers and a few backers. Eventually, when the firm grows and new shares are issued to raise additional capital, its shares will be publicly traded." Excuse me, but there's a 99.9% chance that a private company will never go public. Further, there is a high likelihood that a student will never be in the position of managing the finances of a large public company.

This chapter explains finance for the rest of us. Let's start by reviewing what we've been taught up to now:

- There is one main public capital market in the U.S., also known as Wall Street
- Corporate finance theory explains behavior of the players in the market
- Every business has one true value, determined by the market
- Capital in the market is efficiently allocated and priced in real time
- Going public is the primary goal of every private business owner

Wall Street is the figurative address of the U.S. public stock exchanges. Academics refer simply to "the market." They then use corporate finance theory to explain behavior of parties in "the market." This, of course, assumes that all player behavior is the same in every facet of "the market." Since public securities are priced in real time, they have one true value. This active trading market means that public capital is priced efficiently and predictably. In fact, Wall Street is like a supermarket of securities: Aisle 4 contains commercial paper, aisle 8 has the high-yield debt, and so on. Once a company's risk is established, it's easy to determine the correct aisle and the right price. Finally, corporate finance assumes that every private owner wishes to play this game of "The Price is Right" by taking his or her company public.

So much for what we've been taught. Now let's consider what we need to know. Private finance is a new field of study that focuses on the unique financial needs of private companies.

Here are the tenets of private finance:

- Capital markets are segmented
- A variety of finance theories explain behavior of the players
- Every private business has dozens of correct values at one time
- Private capital is not efficiently allocated and priced
- More companies will go private than public in the foreseeable future

Segmented Capital Markets

Private business is conducted in multiple capital markets. Capital markets are segmented based on a number of factors, including annual revenues, the return expectations of investors, capital access and costs, and mechanisms and institutions. Chapter 1 described market segmentation by annual sales and acquisition multiples into small business, lower-, middle-, and upper-middle market, and large company divisions. Acquisition multiples range, on average, from two to three times EBITDA for a small business to more than 12 times EBITDA for a large company.

Why are markets segmented this way? Well, valuation is essentially an attempt to balance risk and return. Investors' attraction to a market is based on how they perceive risk and return in that market. Those perceptions shape the market, and while owners feel the effects of those perceptions, they are often at a loss to explain what is happening. One of the effects of this shaping is that pricing boundaries appear. For example, IBM, which is typically valued by Wall Street at 20 or so times its earnings, will pay only a six to seven times multiple for a lower-middle market company it wants to acquire. Of course, IBM could pay as much 20 times earnings and still derive value from the deal, but it (correctly) views smaller companies as riskier investments than larger ones and thus requires higher returns from its acquisition.

So why is market segmentation so important? Because the conceptual tools needed to make good decisions about value, capital structure, and business transfer are designed to work in some market segments and not in others. The ability to raise capital for a business, for example, is substantially different in each market segment. A small business will have few capital alternatives while a middle market company in the same industry will have many. Understanding segmentation is vital to developing an appropriate business strategy.

Finance Theory

You might be surprised to learn that what's needed to sort all of this out is good financial theory. Most people are uncomfortable with the word "theory." Einstein is more than likely to blame for this: His theory of relativity ($E=MC^2$) is beyond the grasp of all but a few of us. If you've ever been stuck in an accounting class, it may seem like time is moving slower than normal – but you'd be hard-pressed to explain why theoretically.

Let's make peace with theory: It's nothing more than a method for trying to explain something. Good theories explain things well; bad theories do it poorly. Now let's apply this to finance. Useful capital market theories explain the behavior of players in a capital market.

But no one theory can do this job, as the following graphic depicts:

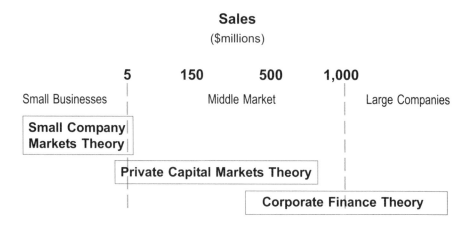

Corporate finance theory was developed in the 1960's to explain the behavior of large companies in the public capital markets. It covers issues such as capital asset pricing, option pricing, agency, and net present value, as well as describing conceptual tools that work in public markets. But the economists who framed corporate finance theory never intended these tools to be used to predict other markets' behavior. Most of it, in fact, is never used by private business owners, nor should it be.

"Small Company Markets Theory" doesn't even exist yet in finance literature. Elements of it are appearing in the form of valuation standards for appraising small business interests, explanation of capital raising constructs, such as the Small Business Administration's programs, and writings on transferring small businesses. At some point in the near future, institutions within the small business market will mature sufficiently to enable the development of an integrated theory, but it hasn't happened yet.

My book, *Private Capital Markets,* has recently introduced private capital markets theory into the literature. As an integrated body of knowledge that applies to valuation, capitalization and transfer of private companies, especially those with annual revenues between $5 million to $500 million, private capital markets theory is designed to help business owners make better financing and investment decisions. The key to understanding private capital markets is to realize that valuation, capitalization, and business transfer all rely on each other for definition and support. Thus, only by understanding each of these areas and their connections is it possible to use this body of knowledge.

Of course, theories are useful only if they can predict as well as explain. Corporate finance theories do not predict behavior in private capital markets; likewise, private capital markets theory is not predictive in the public markets. However, the right financial theory can give business owners a competitive advantage.

One Value, or Many?

The ancient Greeks were consumed with the idea of the one and the many. Was there one river, or were there many water molecules? Should one bad person be extinguished for the good of the many? Thousands of years later, I have a question for you: Is there one true value for every business, or are there many?

Assuming Einstein was correct and time is relative, then there's no reason why private business valuation can't also be relative. In fact, valuations of a private business can differ wildly depending on the reason for the appraisal. Private securities do not enjoy access to an active trading market and real-time pricing. Therefore, to obtain a valuation, either a private appraisal must be undertaken or a transaction must occur. Either method determines the value of a private company *only for a particular reason at a particular point in time.*

The reason for obtaining a valuation governs the selection of a *value world*. Each value world has specific rules and methods that are used to determine how the valuation is obtained. Each value world also has one or more authorities dictating those rules and methods.

Consider this example: Business owners are the ultimate authority in the *Owner* value world – their valuation is gospel. If an owner claims his business is worth $10 million, it is, at least in that world. Now suppose the managers want to buy the business. They are operating in the *Investor* value world. As investors, they are the authorities in their world and they can only pay what the capital markets will give them. There are as many value worlds as there are reasons for an appraisal, each with a different authority setting the rules: for example, Collateral value (secured lenders); Fair Market value (the IRS, courts); Insurable value (insurance companies); Bankruptcy value (judges, federal law); and Early Equity value (venture capitalists).

Because each value world is likely to set a different price for a business interest, private business valuation is a range concept. Thus, a private business interest has *at least* as many correct values at a given point in time as the number of value worlds in which it can be judged. How does a deal ever happen if parties are valuing a business in different worlds? In this case, the parties may meet and negotiate in a neutral world, say the *Market* value world. If the parties are unwilling to haggle it out or respect the authority in that world, the investment bankers, no deal will occur.

A private owner should never try to raise capital or transfer a business without first knowing the company's value. To do so would be the business equivalent of flying blind. Without a current valuation, owners don't have a clue how much their business could be worth.

The Bizarre Bazaar of Private Capital

In any value world, a private business value is influenced by the company's access to capital, because without capital, a business can neither grow nor sustain its current financial position. With no well-organized market, private capital is distributed on a deal-by-deal basis in a setting that's more like an outdoor bazaar than a supermarket.

And what a bizarre bazaar it is. Imagine that merchants withheld from flea market shoppers two critical pieces of information: the price of the goods and the qualifications necessary to buy them. We've all been to a flea market and had to dicker on price, so the first unknown may not deter us. Not knowing if you qualify to buy the goods, which is what happens in private capital markets, is another matter altogether. Capital shopkeepers, be they banks, asset-based lenders, mezzanine investors, or private equity funds, neither post prices for their capital nor typically announce the characteristics the borrower must possess to access their money. Worse, they are constantly moving around and may or may not rely on prior transactions to make current decisions.

So what's a borrower to do? The answer: try to find out how each provider comes to a decision. Although it's not disclosed, every capital source has a "credit box", which describes the criteria necessary to access their capital. For example, most banks are cash flow talkers but collateral lenders. Their credit box is based mostly on the collateral position of the borrower. On the other end of the capital spectrum, venture capitalists' credit boxes are highly dependent on management talent, growth opportunities for the business, and their ability to exit it. My book, *Private Capital Markets*, lists credit boxes for all major capital sources in the U.S.

To balance their risk, capital providers expect to receive certain returns on their capital. These rates of return consider all of the terms of the investment, so it is not enough for a borrower to look just at the stated interest rate on a loan, for instance. Origination costs, compensating balances and monitoring fees can all add to the cost of borrowing that money. Once a business owner knows the full cost, it's possible to compare different types of capital on the same basis and thereby make an informed decision.

Remember that creating value means generating returns that exceed your cost of capital. Owners have to know their company's cost of capital and develop strategies to minimize that cost and maximize the return.

Business Transfer as a Private Choice

Conventional wisdom says that most private business owners dream of taking their companies public. But for the foreseeable future, more public companies will go private each year than vice versa. This is true for several reasons. First, it no longer makes economic sense to be a small public company. The Sarbanes-Oxley law alone adds compliance costs that are prohibitive for many businesses. Second, unless a public company has a float – the market value of all outstanding shares — of at least $300 to $400 million, the major investment banks won't make a market for its stock. Without a market, the stock's liquidity is limited. Third, capital is now plentiful for private companies. This removes one of the principal reasons many companies go public. Finally, a plethora of transfer options now exist for private owners, meaning most can generate or pass along wealth and still remain private — even if they don't sell the business.

Once again, the owner's motive determines how the transfer ultimately occurs. Owners motives fall into one of seven transfer channels: Employees; Charitable trusts; Family; Co-owners; Outside – retire; Outside – continue; and, Go Public. For instance, owners who wish to transfer their business to their children choose the Family transfer channel. Owners who desire to transfer the business to an outsider and then retire choose the Outside - retire channel.

Each transfer channel contains numerous transfer methods. A transfer method is the actual technique used to transfer a business interest. Employee stock ownership plans (ESOPs), family limited partnerships, and buy-sell agreements are all examples of transfer methods. Here's a critical insight: Transfer methods correspond to specific value worlds! For instance, transferring stock into an ESOP occurs in the Fair Market value world, while selling stock via an auction happens in the Market value world. Why the connection? Because an authority says so!

To recap: An owner's motive for a transfer leads to the choice of a transfer method, and the transfer method can occur in only one value world. Each value world employs a unique appraisal process that yields a particular value. In other words, owners ultimately *choose* the value at which they transfer their business. Not a bad deal, right?

Owner Motives Matter Most

As you can see, in any valuation, it's the business owner's motives that matter most. Motives initiate action; they are the key that turns the ignition. Motives without the means to carry them out, however, is a problem that has long haunted private business owners. Historically, owning a private business was not unlike owning a family farm: so few options existed to exit the business that owners could only hope their wives bore them sons. Fortunately, this situation has greatly improved in the past 10 years or so. Motives and means are now matching up.

Let's briefly review the importance of motives. The motives of various players determine the reason for a business appraisal, which determines the value world in which the valuation will occur. Owner motives also determine the types of capital that comprise a company's capital structure and the cost of that capital. For example, many owners refuse to share equity. Other owners will only grow their business as fast as the bank will allow. Finally, an owner's motives dictate how the business is transferred. Once they make the choice of method, the owner has also chosen the value at which the business will transfer.

Of course, owners must be informed before motives can be acted upon. This leads to the key insight regarding private finance: Once a business owner knows what he or she wants to accomplish and understands the structure of the private capital markets, the financial resources are available to support their needs. In other words, the means are there to meet the owner's motives.

Part II

ARBITRAGE

Arbitrage 101

Arbitrage is my favorite word in the English language. It's actually French in origin. Roughly translated, it means "riskless profit." Now I ask you: Is there any better profit that one can earn?

Of course, in the pursuit of profit, you can never eliminate risk altogether. Arbitrage strategies simply take advantage of inter-market imbalances between risk and return. Here's a real world example. Years ago, Coors sold its beer only in the Western United States. This enforced scarcity made Coors extremely desirable in the Eastern half of the country. So a few enterprising businesspeople would buy it out West and ship it to bars in New York and Boston — at an obscene profit, of course. By identifying and exploiting a market imbalance they were able to create an arbitraged return.

Properly implemented, arbitrage strategies enable a manager who understands how markets work to reap a return greater than the underlying risk of the investment. In that way, the manager creates value.

A risk/return imbalance is normally achieved one of three ways:

- Increasing return without increasing risk
- Decreasing risk without decreasing return
- Increasing market position without a corresponding increase in risk

Successful arbitrage relies on exploiting some advantage. A company's advantage can result from any number of conditions. One company might use resources more effectively than the competition while another boasts a superior knowledge of markets, another better understands and predicts the behavior of other players, and another is more able to benefit from capital market segmentation. Every advantage, no matter what it is, creates an opportunity to achieve arbitraged returns. The next six chapters contain stories of Midas Managers who have identified their advantage and created and implemented successful arbitrage strategies to exploit it.

Chapter 6: A Valuable View

You can't create value in a business until you generate a return in excess of your cost of capital. This is news to most private business owners, many of whom don't even know their company's cost of capital. Every type of capital has an "all-in" cost — this is the full cost of the loan, not just the stated interest rate — and it typically varies by market segment. For example, small companies normally pay 30 to 40% for equity capital while middle market companies might only have to pay 20-30%. Yet a small company could be viewed by equity investors as a mid-sized company and still receive the higher returns typical of its market segment. How is this possible? Because top performing companies are often viewed as less risky than similar-sized but lower-performing counterparts and thus can receive higher acquisition multiples or pay a lower cost for capital.

Chapter 7: The Corporate MBO Game

Large corporations are always divesting non-core divisions. In many cases, these divestitures are the result of a change in the parent company's strategic direction rather than dissatisfaction with the performance of the division. And while corporations are fairly effective at selling divisions with annual sales above $100 million, they're not as good at finding buyers for smaller units. This arbitrage strategy allows a manager (and his or her co-investors) to purchase assets on the cheap in the hopes of eventually selling them at a higher price. When the parent company has reasons for selling other than pure financial gain, the buyer can often achieve an arbitraged return.

Chapter 8: Selling the Same Business Twice

This is the have-your-cake-and-eat-it-too strategy known as an equity re-capitalization, or recap. An owner sells part of the equity her equity in the company in order to "take some chips off the table" but continues to operate the business. Recaps can involve the sale of any amount of company stock, but usually there is a change of control. First, a sale is made to an institutional investor, then four to fives years later, the stock is sold on the open market. This strategy enables an owner to reduce the risk of ownership and still benefit from future upside.

Chapter 9: The Buyin – Buyout Game

Let's say an owner no longer wants to manage his business but doesn't want to sell it for another three to five years. In this strategy, the owner sells an option to someone who would eventually like to own the business and is capable of running it in the meantime. Normally the exercise price on the option is set at a level higher than what the company could reasonably fetch at the time it is granted. This strategy enables the owner to retire now and limit his exit risk by locking in an acceptable return.

Chapter 10: The Consolidation Math Game

Bigger is typically better, at least when it comes to acquisition multiples. The larger the company, the larger the multiple it receives when it sells. Small companies typically sell for two to three times earnings, mid-sized companies usually sell for four to six times, and large companies should sell for more than 10 times earnings. If a company wants to eventually realize a higher selling multiple, it may choose to consolidate its way there. This strategy works best when the acquirer pays multiples lower than the multiple implied by its own current valuation. In that way, a mid-sized company acquiring small companies could eventually command a large-company multiple. This creates an arbitraged return.

Chapter 11: The Midas Mentor

Midas Managers who guide other business owners to their financial goals are called Midas Mentors. Their involvement typically reduces the risk of business ownership because the Mentor has already experienced — and may have overcome — the critical issues facing the company. In other words, Mentors help owners get over the next wall, often by leading them through the necessary but painful process of re-conceptualizing their business.

Arbitrage strategies are available to all business owners. However, owners should try only those that make intuitive sense for their businesses. Typically, an appropriate arbitrage strategy presents itself to an owner with the following thought: "We're already doing something similar to that strategy. Now we can finish what we started." As the strategy unfolds, the owner's internal compass will be the best guide through the wealth-creation woods.

INVESTMENT BANKER MAN

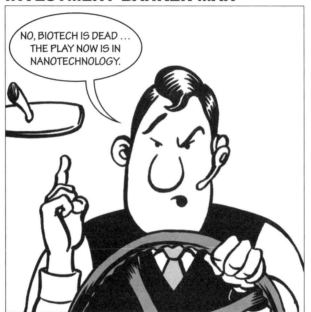

Potentially bigger fools have been identified

6

A Valuable View

AN ARBITRAGE STRATEGY

Norris Jetton knew how to create business value. He had already done it twice in his lifetime, once in his early thirties and again in his early forties. He made his first fortune starting and then selling a company that provided printing services to the packaging industry. He made a second starting and then selling a specialty software company.

What made Norris' wealth creation even more impressive was he had done it with small companies. Neither of his businesses ever achieved more than $6 million in annual sales yet they fetched around $10 million apiece when he sold them. That success led to a nickname: Norris the Niche.

Now Norris the Niche was at it again, hoping to work his wealth-creating magic a third time. His new company, American Pipe Insulation (API), would install a special line of products for sealing and insulating industrial piping. Norris had discovered the sealants by chance while he and his wife, Sheila, were vacationing in Europe. When he returned home, he bought the rights to use the products in the United States under the name ThermoPipeSeal, a name he chose because of the sealants' ability to hold up even under high heat and intense pressure.

Soon, Norris had hired a consulting firm to study which markets would be most receptive to the product's unique sealing properties. While

ThermoPipeSeal could be used in a variety of industries, Norris the Niche decided to target a couple of depressed markets: coal-burning electrical plants and textile manufacturing factories. Norris' friends were not surprised he would choose customers that everyone else was running away from. He had always gone against the grain, and this time would be no different. He was content to let others sell to high-flying industries like beverages and pharmaceuticals. Competition would force their prices down, leaving them with commodity returns, he reasoned.

The lack of competition and potential for solid returns weren't the only factors that attracted Norris. He also liked the planning and installation cycles of the industries he chose. Fossil-fuel plants typically shut down for maintenance for a week or two in the spring and fall of each year, textile plants during the summer. API would generate nearly all of its revenues during these three times of the year.

The sales goal: $6 million per year split 60-40 between utilities and textiles. But Norris knew from his prior successes that sales alone did not drive market value. He would have to focus on other issues if he wanted to create wealth once again. To maximize his equity position, Norris needed to institutionalize his intellectual capital. This meant that he had to:

- Organize API around a transparent business model
- Create recurring and predictable revenue and income streams
- Establish a management structure that would quickly make him superfluous
- Implement systems to generate and manage information effectively
- Own API's intellectual capital but outsource most other operations
- Perform a level of service within API's niche that would enable high profits

Norris focused on meeting these six goals. He knew intuitively that he was trying to get API viewed as a middle-market company instead of the small business that it was. This was a valuable view, since it promised better and cheaper access to capital and a host of transfer options at higher valuations if the business could hit those targets. This arbitraged return would give Norris and API the best of both worlds.

Organize Around a Transparent Business Model

Norris believed that the way a company plans, organizes, and controls to meet its goals determines success or failure in business. API's business plan would need to describe clearly how and from whom it would make money. Norris referred to this as business model transparency because he wanted his key managers and other stakeholders to be able to see clearly the critical success factors affecting the business. Norris learned early in his business career that the more transparent the business model you have, the simpler it is to delegate to managers who can then create value.

API's business model was simple and straightforward. Norris identified the utilities and textiles industries as able to benefit immediately from the sealing properties of ThermoPipeSeal. Through some basic calculations he determined roughly how many facilities in the U.S. could be customers. He also determined that the current insulating products available to those customers were far inferior to his. Thus, the value proposition (the value that his service would create for customers) would enable API to create wealth for itself. Because plant shut-downs were planned a year in advance, he even knew precisely when the customers would need his services.

The API business model followed six simple steps:

1. Identify facilities that could use ThermoPipeSeal and market directly to them.
2. Establish API as the service provider at least three to four months before each plant shutdown.
3. Execute long-term contracts with customers.
4. Price API's solution at 15 percent below market (this still generated a 60 percent gross margin).
5. Outsource as much of the work as possible.
6. Constantly refine and improve the installation process.

Following this business model, Norris believed he could meet his business goals.

Create a Recurring Revenue Stream

Thanks to Norris' sharp focus, API quickly signed long-term contracts with six large customers. Although detailed pricing had to be worked out on a job-by-job basis, the company typically experienced no more than a 10 percent variance from revenues it expected on each shutdown. Thus, Norris could estimate API's annual revenues at the beginning of the year and he could grow the business at his leisure (since his model was scalable, i.e., there were no internal constraints to expanding sales). By the end of the third year, API had $6.5 million in recurring revenues.

Establish an Effective Management Structure

Norris went into every business with the goal of working himself out of a job by the end of the first year. He could probably make himself redundant sooner than that, but he liked living through all seasons of a business at least once before relinquishing day-to-day management.

At the beginning of Year 2, API was essentially being managed by two people. Norris had replaced himself with a seasoned general manager who negotiated all customer and vendor contracts and was responsible for managing the company's working capital (API outsourced most of its financial functions, so it didn't need a full-time controller). The other key manager was the head of operations, who trained and oversaw the supervisors. API employed six or seven supervisors in a year, which meant the Company was generating more than $6 million in sales with no more than 10 full-time employees.

Norris picked employees who possessed three key traits. First, they had to be honest. There was no wiggle room on this. Second, they had to exhibit a lifelong habit of pleasing customers. Finally, they had to be motivated by money.

To satisfy this last trait, Norris shared the company's profits with all full-time employees. The key managers were put in a key person pool, meaning they received 10 percent of API's operating profits split 60/40 between the general manager and the head of operations. The remaining employees split 6 percent of operating profits based on their annual pay. Norris used operating profits as the measurement because it was a level of earnings his employees could affect. He was responsible for "below-the-line" expenses, such as borrowing costs, his compensation, and distributions. Paying out 16 percent of operating profits assured Norris that all of his employees kept his ownership interest in mind.

Implement Effective Systems

Companies with simple business models usually require simple information systems. API could be managed effectively by reviewing just two reports. First was the job book. It listed every job along with the name of the responsible supervisor. All manpower and resource planning was accomplished using the job book. Second, but no less important, was the job cost report. It showed the budget for each job compared with actual costs. The responsible supervisor had to explain any variances. The information needed to prepare these reports was so basic that API could generate it using an off-the-shelf computer program.

Control – Don't Own – the Process Chain

Norris had no desire to own API's process chain, the set of activities required to supply its service. He wanted to own only the intellectual capital and merely control the rest. The following schematic depicts API's process chain:

Market & Sell ThermoPipeSeal ⇨ Order Materials ⇨ Perform Installation ⇨ Invoice & Collect

Norris understood that the only step in this process chain API needed to own outright was the first one. Marketing and selling ThermoPipeSeal depended on API's intellectual capital, or know-how. Understanding customer needs and how to service them were skills that API needed to develop itself and own independently.

Everything else, to one degree or another, could be outsourced. The general manager negotiated all supply contracts at the beginning of the year based on the job book. Throughout the year, a part-time employee ordered materials on a job-by-job basis. While an API supervisor oversaw installations, local, third-party crews did all of the work. On most jobs, API didn't even own the trucks and tools they used. An outside controller handled all invoicing and accounting. By outsourcing much of its process chain, API was able to employ a highly variable cost structure. Thus, its fixed expenses were quite low, which allowed API to earn high returns.

Make a Bunch of Money

Norris had a philosophy: "Why work hard for $1 when you can work smarter and earn $10?" Everyone at API eventually learned the benefits of this credo. Take a look at the company's income statement in its third year of operations:

Insulation Services, Inc.
Summarized Income Statement

Revenues	$6,500,000
Gross Margins	60%
SG&A	1,850,000
Operating Income	$2,050,000

API's selling, general and administrative expenses (SG&A) included salaries of $400,000 for the two key managers and $100,000 for each supervisor and fringe benefits for all employees totaling $350,000. Outsourced services and miscellaneous costs, including $100,000 to rent a building owned by a company Norris controlled, made up the remaining SG&A.

The Payoff

Even after paying bonuses (a total of $200,000 for key managers and $120,000 for the seven supervisors), Norris was able to distribute more than $1.5 million to himself at the end of Year 3. But he was getting restless.

Norris had always been better at building companies than he was at owning them. A different manager would have worried about doubling API's sales or boosting its profit margins incrementally. Not Norris: He was a creator and harvester of value. Now, he had met his goals for the company and it was time for him to move on to the next opportunity. He wanted to sell API, and he already had a buyer in mind: his managers. They had earned the opportunity.

From the beginning Norris wanted API to be viewed as a middle market company. He thought he had achieved that goal, and now it was time for the payoff. As a small company, API would be worth three to four times recast operating profits, or about $6 million (3.5 times $1.7 million). However, Norris knew that he had built a company with a transparent and easily understood business model, recurring and predictable revenue and earnings, a lean and effective management structure, a rationalized process chain, and a cost structure that allowed for obscenely high earnings.

Norris settled on a non-negotiable price of $10 million, which he reached by multiplying $1.7 million (recast operating profits less bonuses) times six, a common middle-market acquisition multiple. The company had no debt so the entire selling price (less Uncle Sam's cut) would go into Norris' pocket. Not bad for three years' work.

But could his managers afford to pay $10 million for the company? Between them they had about $500,000 in equity. This left them short $9.5 million. Yet the same reasons that made Norris believe API was worth so much were now working in his managers' favor. A cash-flow lender offered to put up $6.5 million, which amounted to more than three times the company's annual cash flow. The managers had created a five-year business plan that promised yearly sales of $15 million and operating profits of almost $5 million. On this basis, they were able to entice a mezzanine investor to lend them the final $3 million.

For the third time in his life, Norris received $10 million from the sale of a business, and he wasn't yet 50 years old. What's more, his managers now owned a great business, the lenders lent to a great business, and the employees worked for a great business. Norris Jetton's valuable view had paid off for everyone involved.

BLUEPRINT

Norris' vision for API started with a niche, a hope and a prayer. He followed it up with smart planning and effective organization that kept the goal of creating wealth at the forefront of everyone's minds. API's story shows that a company does not have to be big to be valuable, and you won't be surprised to learn that Norris is now building his fourth small business in very much the same way.

Arbitrage brought API returns that were greater than its underlying risk. Getting the market to view your company on a lower-cost capital market line can do this. It is possible for a small business, for instance, to be viewed as a lower-middle market company even if it is still generating the higher returns that the small market promises.

How is this best-of-both-worlds scenario possible? Companies that perform at the top of their industry are usually viewed as less risky than their under-performing counterparts. This explains why some companies fetch much higher acquisition multiples or lower-cost capital than their similarly-sized competitors. In other words, investors and sources of capital believe these winners play on a less risky capital market line than might be indicted by their diminutive size.

Here are some specific steps you can take to replicate this strategy:

1. Create a transparent business model for your company. That simply means organizing all of your company's activities around customer needs and filling those needs in an efficient way. When anyone can understand the business, the risk goes down dramatically. To test if a business model is transparent, try explaining it to a 14-year old. If a teenager can understand it, it's probably simple enough to launch.

2. Strive to create recurring and predictable revenue and income streams. If a contractor like API can accomplish this, then most companies should be able to do it. And note that it's not always necessary to get customers to sign long-term contracts; it's often sufficient to get customers "hooked" on your company's products or services such that they could not imagine buying anywhere else. Carving out a place in the market, a niche that you can defend, has this effect. This is why managers of private companies need to be niche-aholics. Just ask Norris the Niche.

3. Think and act strategically. Like Norris, most Midas Managers want to delegate day-to-day operating work to others as quickly as they can. That's because they know they can create more value making and implementing strategic plans than they can installing insulation. To this end, the goal of every business owner should be to ascend to the role of Active Chairman.

4. Information is power, so treat it that way. Unsuccessful companies are constantly surprised — by trends in the market, by changes in customer behavior, by their own mistakes, and so on. Successful owners are rarely surprised. They always strive to have a good handle on information and good systems in place that will give it to them.

5. Rationalize your company's process chain. These words might seem foreign to private business owners and managers, but in an 24/7/365 global economy, everything a company does to provide its goods or services should be outsourced if it isn't adding value. Intellectual capital is always owned by the company; the rest of the chain need only be controlled.

Possessing a valuable view generates value for a company on its own, even if an owner decides never to sell the business. Good businesses are easier and more fun to operate than poor ones and top performers attract top talent to continue the virtuous cycle. This chapter illustrates the thought process and actions of an owner who starts businesses with a common motive: to create wealth. Regardless of the industry, he achieves his goal because he employs the same strategy each time. The best news: His valuable view and the arbitrage strategy to achieve it can work for anyone.

The Corporate MBO Game

AN ARBITRAGE STRATEGY

Terry Lancaster had just hung up from a phone call that would change his life. On it, his boss had explained that Terry's division was about to be divested, part of a broader restructuring within its parent company. But the boss said if Terry was patient and kept his head down, everything would work out.

Patience was a virtue Terry had in great abundance. He had long ago adopted the practice of listening and learning before acting. Terry had spent nearly 20 years toiling in the engineering and sales ranks before being promoted to general manager of Super Films, a manufacturer of specialty acrylic films. In five years, Terry had doubled the division's sales to $30 million and more than quadrupled profits. He had hoped this success would lead to a group manager position, a launching pad to eventually running the multi-billion-dollar, publicly held parent company.

The phone call had changed those plans, but it wasn't exactly a surprise. The parent company had changed CEOs about six months before, and the new boss was not a films guy. He planned to re-allocate resources to areas he knew best and divest divisions that, while core to the parent's success for more than a decade, were now superfluous. In all, 10 divisions would be sold off. Terry's was the smallest of these, but also the fastest-growing.

In short order, the parent company hired a Wall Street investment bank to sell the non-core divisions. Terry wrote the selling memorandum for the junior banker assigned to Super Films and prepared a one-hour presentation to show prospects. Terry also gave the investment banker the names of eight or 10 companies that might have a strategic interest in acquiring his division. Several months later, a handful of private equity investors visited, but no strategic buyers ever set foot in the plant. Terry later discovered that none had ever been contacted.

Super Films was a niche player, and interacted very little with its sister companies. With other divisions drawing much more interest from the market, it was beginning to look like the ugly stepchild. Within a year, eight of the 10 divisions had buyers, but Terry's company hadn't drawn any offers, nor was it likely to. The parent had already taken a write-off and the CEO was anxious to remove all non-core assets from the balance sheet prior to the next analyst meeting, which was only three months away.

Terry was asked to visit headquarters to meet with the parent's chief financial officer. Terry worried that the parent company might be ready to close Super Films, but he knew that was unlikely. The division yielded almost $4 million per year in EBITDA. Instead, the CFO shocked Terry by asking if he would consider buying it himself. He told Terry that the parent would sell it to him for a "fair price." Terry did not know what a fair price was, or how to determine one. But he did know his division had substantial value, so putting a deal together would be in his best interest. Terry said he would think about it and get back to him in a few days.

Time was on his side. With no other buyers in the picture and an antsy CEO, Terry could swing a favorable deal. And his weak financial position was actually a strength. The CFO suspected that Terry had little money to invest, a fact that Terry repeatedly confirmed. His $200,000 per year salary certainly didn't allow him to build a nest egg beyond his house and 401k.

Terry hatched a plan to use his apparent financial naiveté and the parent's time sensitivity to his advantage.

The following week the CFO called to see if Terry had thought about the management buyout they had discussed. Terry had a hunch that the CFO had been instructed to make a deal happen - and fast. The parent company had more than $15 million invested in the division, but receiving a return on that investment was not the driving factor here.

Terry had been doing his homework in an attempt to figure out the game and he felt ready to play. However, he decided to let the CFO "guide" him through the buyout process.

Terry answered that he was interested in buying Super Films but didn't know how to proceed. The CFO told Terry that the deal price and structure would be based on the amount of money and terms that various capital players would put up. As a starting point, the CFO introduced Terry to the parent's banker, who reviewed Super Films' balance sheet. The banker calculated the division's collateral value as follows:

Super Films Collateral Value

($000)

Asset Class	Stated Value	Lendable Value/ Fair Market Value	Advance Rate	Margined Collateral Value
Accounts Receivable	$2,722	2,500	80%	$2,000
Inventory	1,450	1,000	50%	500
Land/Building	2,442	2,000	70%	1,400
Machinery & Eqpt.	1,866	1,500	65%	975
Total				$5,000

The *Stated Value* for each of the asset classes was taken from Super Films' balance sheet. The *Lendable Value/Fair Market Value* column showed the amounts eligible for secured lending: Accounts Receivable was reduced to reflect ineligible receivables, such as past due invoices or those generated from related companies; Inventory was reduced to account for work-in-progress, which was not eligible for lending; Land and Building and Machinery and Equipment were both adjusted to their fair market values.

The banker explained that the *Advance Rate* was the percentage of the Lendable or Fair Market Value in each asset class that his bank could actually let him borrow. For example, the bank would advance 80% against eligible receivables, 50% against eligible inventory, and so on. *Margined Collateral Value* was the sum of the margined property in each asset class. For Super Films, margined collateral value totaled about $5 million. The banker offered to lend Terry $4.6 million on the condition it was senior debt, i.e., the bank received a first lien on all of the division's assets.

The CFO wasn't done finding capital for Terry's buyout. Next he introduced him to the bank's mezzanine capital representative. She explained that mezzanine capital was subordinated debt that provided borrowing capability on top of senior debt with less of the dilution of ownership associated with equity capital. Since it ranked behind senior debt for purposes of principal and interest repayment, mezzanine capital carried more risk for the lender and consequently would be more expensive for him to borrow.

The mezzanine banker offered 1.5 times EBITDA for the buyout, or about $6 million. Repayment of principal was deferred for two years, which would help Terry meet his cash flow projections, but, as expected, the capital came at a steep price. With help from his advisors, Terry figured his all-in cost was nearly 23%. This was comprised of a 12% coupon, or interest rate, and something called "warrants." A warrant was a right to buy a security at a fixed price, also known as the exercise or strike price. The bank's mezzanine deal included *detachable* warrants, which, after four years, could be repurchased by the borrower at a pre-defined price. The mezzanine representative quoted a price of 6 times the company's EBITDA at the time of exercise times 5%. Terry figured that would be about $4 million at the end of the fourth year — on top of the interest and principal on the $6 million loan!

The CFO was working hard and had the cash for Terry's down payment up to $10.6 million ($4.6 million from secured bank loan; $6 million from mezzanine). But he wasn't done yet. He figured he could get another $5 million added to the purchase price by involving an institutional investor. He introduced Terry to a private equity group (PEG) that specialized in backing management buyouts. This particular PEG had developed a method for enticing managers into a deal by making their money worth more than its *pro rata* share. After several meetings, the PEG offered to let Terry buy 20% of the shares of Super Films for $300,000. Further, if Super Films hit its financial targets, Terry would *earn-in* another 2% per year over five years.

Including this newfound equity, the CFO had the purchase price up to $15.6 million. There was only one problem: Terry wasn't going to play the CFO's game. He wasn't going to use the parent's bank for the secured loan or the mezzanine capital, and he wasn't going to bring in partners who would control his financial future. Terry had a different idea.

More than a month had passed since the CFO first contacted Terry about acquiring the division. Terry could tell that the pressure was building at headquarters to dump Super Films. Terry decided now was a good time to take a forceful step, so he took an extended vacation to the Caribbean. After returning rested and tanned, he was asked by the CFO to stop by so they could get going with the deal.

Terry thanked the CFO for arranging the meetings with the various capital sources and for taking such an interest in his well-being. Then he laid out the deal he had in mind. The CFO knew that he'd been had when Terry said he'd get the down payment from an asset-based lender, not the parent's bank. "A damn sight smarter than I thought he was," the CFO said to himself.

Terry had figured out that a bank is a great place to get money, but only if you don't need it. Asset-based lenders are more concerned with collateral than a borrower's cash balance or future profitability, and Terry was willing to pay an extra point in interest to get this flexibility. Because of the asset-based lender's aggressive advance policy, Terry was able to offer $5 million as a down payment.

Terry hadn't warmed up to the idea of paying the bank 23% for the use of its mezzanine capital, either. The return was too great for the risk. Instead, Terry offered this bridge-financing role to the parent company in the form of a subordinated seller note. He believed the parent would look favorably upon this idea because its only alternative was shutting down the division, which would be bad for publicity and prevent it from recouping most of its investment. So Terry asked for $5 million at 8% with no interest for the first two years and the principal and interest amortizing over the next seven years. And unlike the mezzanine capital, Terry would not personally guarantee the seller note.

Finally, Terry did not want private equity partners in the deal. The guys from the PEG had an MBA smell to them, a definite negative in his book. But he did want partners. Terry told the CFO that he had offered his two top lieutenants a chance to become minority owners of Super Films and both had said yes without hesitating.

Terry knew he was proposing taking away more from this deal than he was offering to the parent, so he played his last card. From his years running the division, Terry knew that story-telling is an important part of any executive's job. So he gave the CFO fodder for a story that he hoped would sell the CEO on his proposal: an earn-out. An earn-out is a method for triggering changes in the purchase price based on the future performance of the company. In other words, it's a "bridge tool" to help buyers and sellers to reach an agreement on the purchase price. In a big corporation, earn-outs can also prevent the messenger who delivers a deal from getting shot by the boss. Terry proposed a two-year earn-out that had the potential of adding a couple of million dollars to the deal. Of course, the CFO would have preferred cash up front from a PEG, but he knew he could sell the earn-out up the ladder. The promise of millions more received from the sale provided good political cover.

This structure couldn't have worked much better for Terry. He had virtually no liquidation risk, since only the debt to the asset-based lender was personally guaranteed. He figured he could sell off the division at any time and make enough to pay off the senior loan. The seller note was easy on cash flow so he would be able to ramp the business up and still meet payroll. Terry even got the CFO to agree to subordinate the parent note to an institutional mezzanine provider should Terry decide to pursue such a financing. Most importantly to Terry, he would own 80% of the new entity (a vast improvement over the PEG deal) and his key managers would own the remaining 20%.

Terry believed he was getting such a good deal because the parent's executives were motivated by non-financial factors. In truth, it was no money out of their pockets if they got less than they had hoped for the division. The main thing was they were getting rid of it. Thus, Terry had sensed a market imbalance and created an arbitraged return for himself and his partners. He expected them to receive a return on their investment that far surpassed the underlying risk. Based on $4 million in EBITDA and a middle market acquisition multiple of five, Terry felt he could flip Super Films to any of a number of competitors for at least $20 million. After paying off the asset-based loan and the seller note, he'd still be $10 million richer.

But Terry chose another path. He grew the business over time and ultimately employed the strategy described in the next chapter – an equity recapitalization - to create both an exit for himself and substantial value for his company. Once again, his patience paid off.

BLUEPRINT

The Corporate MBO Game requires good timing, a fair amount of patience, and luck. There are opportunities to play this game in almost any type of economy, but understanding that the transfer market is cyclical can be quite beneficial. The following chart shows the typical 10-year market cycle for private company transfers.

Ten Year Private Company Transfer Cycle

Years

1	3	8	10
Deal Recession (Buyer's Market)	**Prime Selling Time** (Seller's Market)	**Almost Deal Recession** (Neutral Market)	

It is no coincidence that the cycle mirrors general macroeconomic activity. Transfer cycles begin with two to three years of deal recession reflecting an economic recession that causes banks and other capital providers to stop making loans and investments. It also causes large companies to focus on their core businesses and curtail aggressive acquisition plans. For managers, this is the best time to play the Corporate MBO Game.

From a seller's perspective, the prime time to sell a business occurs during the middle years of the transfer cycle. During these years, capital is available to buyers to finance deals and the MBA crowd has convinced Wall Street to start funding roll-ups and other consolidations again. Big companies are back in the game, too, hungry to grow their income statements and balance sheets through strategic acquisitions.

The smartest sellers typically wait until near the end of the seller's market before making a move. This offers them the benefits of increased profitability during the good years plus the highest transfer pricing.

Economic storm clouds start forming again about eight years into the 10-year cycle. This economic uncertainty ultimately leads to another deal recession, and the cycle starts all over again.

Deal periods in a transfer cycle do not start and stop like binary switches. They're more like leaky faucets. Opportunities exist in every period. However, the best time for a manager to play the Corporate MBO Game is without question during a buyer's market.

There are a number of steps managers can follow to play this game effectively. Some key considerations to keep in mind:

1. This strategy works best when a large company is divesting a small division. Pay attention to happenings at the parent company, especially changes in strategic direction that could affect the fate of the division you want to buy.

2. If you're trying to play this game during a recession, make sure you will have enough cash to survive post-deal. Although the acquisition price is often the best during these periods, buying early in a recession can presage cash flow problems later.

3. Be patient once a parent decides to divest. The MBO Game is a reactive, not proactive, strategy. Avoid auctions or any other selling process that pits you against the market of investors. This game is all about playing off ego and paternalism at headquarters.

4. Once the intent to divest the division to the managers is made clear, the lead manager should form a team of advisors. At the very least, it should include a corporate lawyer, a CPA, and an investment banker. But let the team stay in the background until after a letter of intent is signed. There's no benefit to showing the parent you know how to play the game in the early rounds.

5. The game officially begins once the negotiations start. The key manager has a critical decision to make at this point: if any other managers will be invited onto the buyout team. As a rule, the fewer, the better, and only those who possess skill sets that can't be hired in the open market should be invited to join. In all, you should have no more than three or four managers on the ownership team.

6. The advisory team can help the lead manager develop a strategy and draft a letter of intent. But avoid the temptation of acting like you know what you're doing when dealing with the parent. With any luck, the parent's representatives will have been instructed to sell the division as quickly as possible.

7. The down payment should consist of whatever can be borrowed from a senior lender. The remainder of the purchase price should consist of seller notes and earn-outs. The goal is to acquire the company for about one-half of its "strategic market value." You should never personally guarantee a seller note.

8. A well thought-out capital structure will enable your company to weather a 12-month downturn. Mr. Murphy — he of "whatever can go wrong, will" — is sure to show up soon after closing, so arranging excess borrowing capacity is essential.

9. Surround yourself with advisors who have already made the transition from professional-manager to owner-manager. This conversion is difficult but it's always easier if you have a seasoned support group.

Managers do not always get a chance at the brass ring. This is because parent companies are often successful selling divisions to outside parties. If the buyer is a competitor, managers may well fear for their jobs. But if the buyer is a private equity group, managers should negotiate an incentive arrangement that will protect them, so even if they can't play the Corporate MBO Game, they can still participate in the future success of the business.

INVESTMENT BANKER MAN

A leading cause of serious rib injuries among bankers

8

Selling the Same Business Twice

AN ARBITRAGE STRATEGY

After nearly ten years, Kelly Johnson was tired of it. "It" was the constant battle she faced financing the growth of her business, Quality Foods.

When she founded the food processing company way back then, she never dreamed it would reach $15 million in annual sales. Along the way, however, she had made tremendous sacrifices, both personally and professionally. She had also financially "bet the ranch" for an entire decade, and that needed to change.

First, though, she needed financing. Based on contracts already on the books, Quality Foods was going to double its sales in the next two years. Kelly knew that about 20 cents in working capital was required to support each new dollar of sales. Thus, she was looking at an additional investment of about $3 million, on top of another $2 to $3 million in capital expenditures to increase Quality's capacity. Although the company was quite profitable, there was no way it would earn enough in the next year or so to cover $5 to $6 million in spending.

Other than the aggravation involved with chasing capital, Kelly still enjoyed the challenges of running Quality Foods. In a perfect world, she would concentrate on growing the company, not raising money. Kelly knew the food business but did not know how to solve her capital quandary. So she reached out to an investment banker who promised to help make it go away.

The banker studied the problem and presented Kelly with three options. First, she could sell the company and work for the new owner. This would get her off the hot seat financially, but it wasn't a maximizing solution, since in all likelihood Quality Foods would be worth substantially more in the future than it was at that moment. Second, she could attempt to sell a minority interest – say 20 percent. This might solve the financial problem, but bringing in a partner would no doubt complicate her life. Finally, she could sell a controlling interest. While this might solve her capital need, it definitely did not appeal to her control-freak personality.

Show Me the Money

Kelly really didn't want to sell her business, at least not yet. She considered this a fall-back position. Quality Foods would finish the year with EBITDA of about $1.5 million. The banker explained to Kelly that the market would pay a multiple of Quality's *recast* EBITDA. Recast simply meant that Quality's income would be increased by the total of all of her discretionary expenses and one-time costs. Kelly supplied the following recast items for the current year:

Quality Foods Recast Items

Seller excess compensation	$150,000
+ Family members on Board of Directors	25,000
+ Loss due to fire	75,000
Recast Total	$250,000

Kelly reasoned that she would be willing to sign an employment agreement with the new owner for compensation of $150,000 per year. Including salary, bonus, and fringes, she was now taking $300,000 per year from the business. The difference of $150,000 was excess compensation that would be available to the next owner. Likewise, two members of Kelly's family sat on Quality's Board of Directors and were paid a total of $25,000 per year. The next owner certainly would not retain their services. Finally, Quality had suffered a small electrical fire during the year which resulted in an uninsured loss of about $75,000. Kelly hoped that this was a one-time expense.

Based on Kelly's workup, the investment banker added back about $250,000 to Quality's reported EBITDA of $1.5 million and arrived at a recast EBITDA of $1.75 million. Buyers would not take Kelly's word for the recast amounts, so she would have to substantiate every dollar. She would need to prove that excess seller compensation of $150,000 was indeed *excess*, for instance.

Once recast EBITDA was determined, the investment banker determined an acquisition multiple. He explained that this multiple was a short-hand way of describing risk. A multiple of five, for example, was as the same as saying the buyer needed to achieve a 20 percent return on investment, since the reciprocal of five is one-fifth, or 20 percent. Each buyer would have his or her own expectation of return. However, the banker believed that the right buyer for Quality Foods would be willing to pay a six multiple. Applying that to the recast EBITDA of $1.75 million suggested that Kelly could sell the company for $10.5 million.

Kelly wondered what this really meant. What did the buyer actually get? The banker explained that a "multiple of recast EBITDA deal" typically included the operating assets of the business (collectible accounts receivable, good inventory, functional M&E). It did not include cash, real estate or other non-operating assets. The buyer would take only the current liabilities that didn't bear interest, such as normalized accounts payable and reasonable accruals. The buyer would not assume any other liabilities, such as current or long-term debt.

Although it wasn't typically spelled out, this type of deal also assumed that transferable assets and liabilities were at *normalized* levels for the company at its current financial position. For instance, normalized accounts payable meant the amount that would be customary to support the cost of sales level in its industry. If Kelly were carrying an extra million bucks of non-customary payables, she would be expected to pay it off. Likewise, if some of the receivables turned out to be uncollectible, she would have to eat those out of the proceeds from the sale.

Quality Foods had little cash on hand and did not own its real estate (Kelly owned it on her own). But Quality did have $3 million in interest-bearing debt on its balance sheet, which the buyer would not take. The banker deducted this debt from the $10.5 million enterprise value to arrive at an equity value of $7.5 million.

As appealing as $7.5 million sounded, Kelly knew that the value of Quality might double in the next few years as the company grew. She couldn't stand the thought of handing this value over to someone else to realize. So she rejected the idea of selling the business and next considered selling a minority interest.

Along for the Ride

The banker explained that selling a minority interest in Quality Foods would be a challenge. The first issue was finding an investor who would buy a small interest in the company. Kelly had two choices: private equity groups (PEGs) and wealthy individuals.

There are more than 5,000 PEGs in the U.S. As a group, they have more than $100 billion to invest. These for-profit entities invest in private companies with the hopes of achieving high returns, typically north of 25 percent. Because they prefer control investments, i.e., ownership positions in excess of 50 percent of the stock of a company, most PEGs would pass at the chance to acquire a 20 percent interest in Quality. The banker was experienced, however, and knew several PEGs that would "take a look" at the investment opportunity. These would not be passive investors. The banker told Kelly that these particular PEGs would want to take an active role in devising and executing Quality's strategic plan.

The banker also knew a dozen or so wealthy individuals who might make the investment. They were more inclined than PEGs to make a long-term passive investment in a private company. Further, since they compared investments in private companies to public stocks, individuals tended expect returns in the 15 to 20 percent range.

The ultimate problem with selling a minority stake revolved around valuation. The banker explained that PEGs and individuals were likely to value Quality by applying a multiple of four or five times recast EBITDA. That produced an enterprise value of between $7 and $8.75 million. More importantly for Kelly, this represented an equity value of just $4 to $5.75 million (after deducting $3 million in debt). Assuming the investor bought 20 percent of the stock, she would raise only $1.15 million on the high end. If the investor bought 49 percent, she would raise $2.82 million at most. In either case, Quality would still not have the $5 to $6 million it needed to grow and Kelly would not have received any money personally from the sale. Further, if she sold 49 percent of the equity of Quality, and the equity value doubled in the next few years, she would be right back where she was now.

Kelly didn't like the first two options. Her only hope seemed to rest with selling a majority interest.

Have Your Cake and Eat it Too

Kelly could barely conceive of giving up legal control of Quality Foods. When it came to ownership issues, she had always told herself that she was either all the way in or all the way out. The "go to work for someone else" boat had left the dock long ago. But she had to admit that neither selling out nor taking a minority partner was a viable option. So Kelly decided to keep an open mind on the strategy that her banker dubbed "selling the same business twice," also known as an equity recapitalization.

In an Equity Recap, Kelly would sell majority control of Quality to an outside investor but continue to run the business. Recaps often involve the sale of 80 percent of the equity, which enables the investor to consolidate the company's tax returns in a holding company. And, the banker explained, PEGs love Recaps because they let them share risk with seasoned managers who still own a portion of the stock and are thus aligned with investor interests. Wealthy individuals don't typically do Recaps, mainly because they require investing boatloads of money and taking an active management role.

The banker said this strategy would allow Kelly to have her cake and eat it too. She would receive a substantial payment for the stock she sold, money that was hers to keep. She would also be released from all personal guarantees on Quality's existing debts and wouldn't have to sign any future ones. The PEG would fund half of the $10 million in growth capital that she figured Quality needed over the next five years and future profits would cover the other half. With no capital worries, Kelly could concentrate on growing the business. At the end of five to six years, Quality would be sold again.

The banker said that if Quality was recapped, Kelly's 20 percent ownership interest could be worth a substantial amount in five or six years. With a fully funded business plan, Quality could generate sales of about $50 million and EBITDA of about $10 million. At that point, Quality would fetch at least six times EBITDA, which would make Kelly's stake worth a cool $12 million (six times $10 million times 20 percent).

Kelly was starting to warm up to this strategy, but she had lots of questions. How much money would she receive at the closing? What control would she have over operation of the business? If the PEG decided not to sell Quality in five years, could she still get out? How much would she earn along the way? Would there be incentives or bonuses for her key people?

The banker knew that many PEGs would be interested in recapping Quality Foods. Even with competition, however, it was unlikely that a PEG would value the company at more than 5.5 times EBITDA right now. Kelly would be responsible for paying off 80 percent of the interest-bearing debt at the closing. Thus, she stood to receive about $5.3 million at the closing (5.5 times $1.75 million times 80 percent - $2.4 million debt payoff).

Even after paying taxes, this would give Kelly financial security, but selling her business just once wouldn't be enough. She was determined to make the Recap work. She would have to sign a multi-year employment agreement, but she would no longer have to guarantee debts; so she was happy to work for $150,000 per year. The banker said that Kelly would probably be part of a key person bonus pool, paying perhaps 10 percent of pre-tax profits each year. All of Kelly's other perks, such as vacation time, health benefits, and car allowance, would remain in place.

The trickier part of the deal would be crafting a shareholder agreement with the PEG. Shareholder agreements set the terms by which shareholders deal with each other. The banker explained that these terms were as important to Kelly as the valuation, reminding her of the old adage, "You set the price, and I'll set the terms." Kelly's instinct was to be clear about the terms they wanted when they went shopping for PEGs. The banker agreed, and drew up a term sheet that contained some of the more important ones.

Tag Along – The controlling shareholder cannot sell its interests unless the buyer agrees to purchase Ms. Johnson's interests at the same price and terms.

Mandatory Buyout in the Event of Death – The Company has an obligation to purchase Ms. Johnson's interests in the event that she dies during the term of this agreement.

Short-term Disability – If Ms. Johnson suffers a short-term disability, she will receive full salary for up to six months even if she is unable to work. If the disability extends beyond six months, it will be classified as long-term.

Mandatory Buyout in the Event of Long-Term Disability – The Company has an obligation to purchase the Ms. Johnson's interests in the event that she suffers a long-term disability. Long-term disability means she is unable to perform her duties as defined in the Employment Agreement for more than six months. For these purposes, disability will be determined by the definition in the disability insurance policy in force at that time. The parties will agree to a definition of disability in case no disability insurance policy is in force at the time of the disabling event.

Dispute Resolution – Disputes between the shareholders will be resolved by arbitration, with both sides paying equally for the services of the American Arbitration Association.

Non-Dilution of Ownership Interest – Ms. Johnson's ownership interest in the Company will not be diluted after the Closing unless she agrees in writing.

Financings – PEG agrees to fund the Company's business plan up to $10 million. This capital can be in the form of senior or junior debts. In both cases, if the debt is directly supplied by PEG, the interest rate and terms must be market rates. Ms. Johnson will not personally guarantee any existing or future debts of the Company.

Management Fees – Management fees to the PEG will be limited to 2 percent of annual revenues.

Corporate Governance – Changes to Ms. Johnson's employment agreement, the shareholder agreement, and Buy/Sell agreement cannot be made without Ms. Johnson's signature.

In truth, that was just a start. The banker knew that other terms would ultimately find their way into the shareholder agreement. There was also the issue of a buy/sell agreement term sheet. A buy/sell agreement controls the events that trigger a buyout, determines who can buy a shareholder's interest, and prices the interests that are bought. This agreement would be important to Kelly for two main reasons. First, if she died or became disabled while the agreement was in force, her shares would be purchased by the company at an agreed-upon price, usually determined by a formula. Second, if five years passed without the company being sold, Kelly could *put*, or sell, her shares to the PEG at a price determined by the same formula.

Once again, the banker created a term sheet laying out the key terms. These would be negotiated at the same time as the valuation and shareholder agreement terms. Some of the issues covered by the buy/sell terms were: 1) triggering events, which included death or long-term disability, voluntary termination, and personal bankruptcy; 2) valuation methodology, which determined the "greater" of a number of different values, including an agreed-upon price, book value, insurance-in-force, and multiple of recast earnings; 3) a put option, so Kelly could sell her shares back to the PEG if they changed their timetable and decided not to sell the company later. The buy/sell terms would protect Kelly and her family from unforeseen or unfortunate events.

The banker rounded up ten different PEGs and gave them Quality's business plan, valuation summary, and shareholder and buy/sell term sheets.

Several pursued the deal to negotiations. Since Quality Foods was a quality company, Kelly was able to pick the one she wanted to partner with at terms very close to what she and the banker had initially drafted.

After she signed the legal documents, Kelly was happy with her decision. She had never been a big believer in the "win-win," but an Equity Recap seemed to give each side what it wanted. Kelly realized that selling the same business twice was eminently better than selling it once.

BLUEPRINT

Equity Recaps are useful strategies for business owners who want to:

1) increase personal liquidity, 2) continue operating their business while maintaining a large equity position, 3) reduce personal risk by eliminating borrowing guarantees, 4) gain access to financial professionals who have experience in growing and exiting from businesses, or 5) have a chance to receive non-dilutive capital for growth. This last point is particularly important. In some Recaps, the original owner's equity stake isn't diluted as more growth money is invested. This is often a key item for the two sides in a Recap to negotiate.

There are now thousands of institutional Recap investors in the U.S. segmented by investment size. Most PEGs focus on Recaps requiring $2 to $10 million, the minimum size for institutional support. Another group of PEGs invests primarily in deals requiring $10 to $100 million. About 100 investment firms participate in transactions larger than $100 million.

The following steps must be followed to replicate this strategy:

1. Most private companies are not good candidates for an equity Recap. This is because of growth, or more precisely, lack of it. To be an attractive Recap prospect, be prepared to show EBITDA growth of at least 15 to 20 percent a year for the foreseeable future.

2. Recap candidates need capable management teams since they will likely experience hyper-growth for several years. Not all managers are prepared for this challenge.

3. A Recap requires a solid business plan. The only thing that should be missing from your plan is the ability to capitalize it.

4. Hire someone knowledgeable about Recaps and market value to perform a valuation on your business. Then consider your financial goals and determine what percentage of the company you are willing to offer to the market.

5. Either you or your representatives should prepare shareholder and buy/sell term sheets. Negotiating these terms is every bit as important as arriving at a valuation.

6. Contact at least eight to 10 PEGs and give them the business plan, valuation, and term sheets. Your goal should be to entice at least two or three into detailed deal discussions.

7. Choose a PEG based on several factors. First, the PEG should have experience recapping other companies. Talk to the managers at some of them and find out how they've been treated. Second, the PEG should share your vision. Finally, and most importantly, the PEG should be a partner you feel you can work with.

Owners need to be rested and ready before implementing a Recap. It's a whirlwind experience. But for those with the right energy, the right company, and the right plan, selling the same business twice is both fun and rewarding.

The Buyin – Buyout Game
AN ARBITRAGE STRATEGY

Sarah Clement had always wanted to own her own business. A 10-year tour at a multinational corporation had led to a partner's position with a regional management consulting firm. After a few years of helping business owners maximize their equity positions, Sarah decided to get serious about becoming her own boss. She planned to use her consulting job to help her identify a company to acquire and negotiate the best possible deal.

Unfortunately, the first year's search proved futile. She didn't uncover anywhere near as many buyout opportunities as she had hoped she would. The few she found were small companies, which typically were not good fits for her skills. She had always been better suited to managing mid-sized businesses. Sarah's other problem was money. After years of saving, she had accumulated $400,000 to invest. It was a lot of money to her, but it didn't seem to buy very much. Yet Sarah was determined to put her abilities and money to work.

Plan of Attack

The first order of business was to develop a process that would yield acquisition opportunities. Sarah decided she needed to take a bold step. She couldn't work full-time as a consultant and find a business to buy. Even though everyone thought she was crazy, she quit her job. But Sarah had a plan. She would attack the market until she found the perfect deal. Then she would propose an unusual buyout structure that she hoped would lead to a sale on her terms.

Sarah actually initiated a three-front war on the market. She registered with numerous intermediaries who might help her find a deal. At the same time she contacted dozens of advisors to business owners, including lawyers, CPAs, and estate planners. Finally, she mounted a marketing campaign aimed at business owners themselves. Given all of this effort, Sarah hoped to find a deal within about six months.

During the past year, Sarah had dealt with three main types of intermediaries: business brokers, M&A intermediaries, and investment bankers. Each group dealt with a different segment of the market.

Business brokers worked with either buyers or sellers of small businesses. Their typical transaction was less than $2 million, and they wanted to sell Sarah dry cleaners and restaurants – businesses she had no interest in buying. M&A intermediaries focused on providing merger, acquisition and divestiture services to middle market companies. The average size transaction for this group varied widely, but was normally above $2 million. Investment bankers specialized in raising the capital that larger businesses needed for long-term growth and giving advice on strategic matters such as mergers, acquisitions, and other transactions.

Since Sarah had only $400,000 to invest, neither of the latter two types of intermediaries was going to show her any deals. Sarah soon realized that she would have to find a deal without an intermediary.

Next up were the professionals. Sarah had been meeting with various advisors to middle market companies since she first got the buyout bug, but she needed to take a more organized approach. She formed an acquisition company, called Clement Management Services. She then created a Board of Advisors. This was not a legal Board of Directors; it was more of an ad hoc advisory group. She invited eight different members to this Board. Several were respected business owners who could introduce her to other owners who were thinking of selling out as well as help her review potential deals. Sarah also invited a partner from a mid-sized law firm that would provide legal and advisory services to CMS before and after the deal. This same strategy was behind the selection of a CPA, a partner in a local estate planning firm, and a commercial banker. Sarah asked each Board member for a handful of contacts whom she could contact for further support. Soon, she had compiled a list of more than 50 professionals.

Sarah created a marketing brochure for CMS that described its mission and her profile and listed the names and affiliations of her Board members. She mailed this brochure to anyone she thought would open the envelope. She set a goal of having breakfast or lunch with five or six of these professionals each week.

Go Direct

With her advisor-campaign in gear, it was time to begin contacting business owners directly. She had heard that owners were bombarded by brokers and other people wanting to buy their businesses, so she needed a unique strategy to get their attention. Fortunately, Sarah had one.

Sarah sent a letter and a marketing brochure to about 30 owners of mid-sized businesses each week. The letter did not follow the standard "I want to buy your business" script. The following is the approach she used:

Date

Dear <Sir or Madam>:

I am an entrepreneur and former partner of a mid-sized consulting firm. I seek to invest and assume a senior leadership role in an established company with $5 to $25 million in annual sales.

My broad background suits me to private company management. My experience includes industrial marketing, sales, planning, product development, finance, manufacturing, and engineering. I have also helped owners of mid-sized companies develop budgets and strategic plans.

Any reasonable and mutually agreeable plan for ownership transition interests me. The ideal arrangement would allow me to make a sizeable investment in your company, learn your business, and help you eventually realize an orderly exit.

The enclosed brochure highlights my objectives, background and references. I will contact you in the coming days to discuss our mutual interests. Thank you in advance for your consideration.

Sincerely,

Ms. Sarah Clement

Sarah's strategy was to "buyin, then buyout" a mid-sized company owner's position. This strategy was based on the premise that most owners do not want to sell their business at the point of first being contacted. Rather, most would prefer to continue to own the business while they plan an eventual exit. For these forward-looking owners, it's even better if another capable person can run the business prior to their exit so they don't have to. Sarah was offering to do just that.

Sarah planned to meet with four to five owners each week. She found that sending out 30 letters, followed up with about 60 phone calls, achieved this goal. Combined with her appointments with professionals, Sarah was meeting with at least 10 individuals each week. Little wonder she had to quit her job to concentrate on buying into a business.

After several weeks, Sarah started to generate deal flow. So much deal flow, in fact, that she needed a system for efficiently filtering the opportunities she was getting. So she drew up a list of criteria that enabled her to make quick decisions about whether or not to pursue a deal. After the second month, Sarah was evaluating three or four opportunities a week. Most didn't come close to her target, however.

Sarah's Wish List — *I want to find a...*

1. Partner whom I like and respect
2. Company that needs my skills to grow
3. Company in which I can purchase at least 10 percent of the stock initially
4. Company that I can eventually leverage to effect a complete buyout
5. Company in an industry with growth potential
6. Company with product or services that I can understand

Sarah's luck changed at the end of the third month.

One of her advisors introduced her to Bob Andrews, a 55-year old owner of a pump distribution and repair company. The company, Pump Supply Inc., had annual sales of more than $8 million. Bob had no children in the business and was hoping to retire and sell it by the time he reached 60. Sarah's visit was timely.

The Deal

After several meetings with Bob, Sarah was convinced she could add value at PSI. Bob was comfortable with Sarah as well. He could envision making her the company's sales manager for the first year. If this went well, she would become chief operating officer by the end of the second year. The only difficulty was determining how to structure the financial relationship.

PSI reported annual EBITDA of about $500,000. Adding back Bob's discretionary expenses yielded a recast EBITDA of $700,000. Bob thought that his business was worth $6 to $7 million, but using what he thought was traditional valuation methodology only got him to $3.5 million ($700,000 times a multiple of five). That was good news for Sarah: she could buy 10 percent of PSI and still have $50,000 in the bank.

But Sarah would only complete the buyin if she could negotiate four agreements with Bob: 1) an employment agreement; 2) a shareholder agreement; 3) a buy/sell agreement; and 4) the purchase of an option to acquire Bob's remaining 90 percent interest at some point in the future.

Agreeing to employment terms was the easiest task. As sales manager Sarah would receive a salary of $100,000 per year plus incentives based on gross profit growth. Her salary would rise to $125,000 once she became COO, and the incentive package would increase proportionately. Sarah negotiated all of the other terms that are often forgotten in these situations: vacation days, use of a company car, dues for membership in a local entrepreneurs club, and so on. Unless she committed a felony or some other major violation of her employment agreement, Sarah would receive a severance equal to 12 months pay if she were to be terminated.

Negotiating the shareholder agreement was a trickier proposition. Sarah would be a minority shareholder in PSI. She had studied the ramifications of this position and knew it created tremendous risk for her. Minority investors live at the whim of the majority. Bob could hire or fire whomever he desired and drain the company's finances if he wished. And plenty of other things that weren't in Bob's control could happen. He might become disabled. He might get divorced, which would distract him from running the business. He might get burned-out to the point of indifference.

To protect her position, Sarah drafted a term sheet that contained typical shareholder and buy/sell agreement provisions (See Chapter 8 for an example).

A buy/sell agreement would describe how Sarah's stake would be valued if a "triggering" event occurred. Triggering events included death or long-term disability of either her or Bob and termination of Sarah. A termination would fall into one of three categories: 1) with cause, if she violated her employment agreement, 2) at will, if Bob fired her without cause, or 3) voluntary, if she quit.

If either Sarah or Bob died or became disabled for more than six months, their shares would be valued using the following formula:

$$\text{Value} = ((\text{Recast EBITDA for the most recent year} * 6) - \text{interest-bearing debt}) * \text{Share \%}$$

Value was determined differently if Sarah was terminated with cause. In this case, her original investment of $350,000 would be discounted by 50 percent and she would get $175,000. If she left the company voluntarily, her original investment would be discounted by 25 percent, or down to $262,500.

With either of these types of termination, she would be paid in equal payments over three years. If Sarah was terminated without cause, she would get her original investment back in full, payable on the day she left the company.

The option agreement was the most difficult to conceive and execute. Sarah's strategy of buying out Bob's position at some point in the future was based on several factors. First, she didn't have enough money, or the ability to raise it, to acquire Bob's shares from the outset. Second, she had never worked in the pump supply industry before and there was some risk that she wouldn't like it or be effective in it. Third, she figured that by the time she actually bought Bob's remaining shares, she would be viewed by capital providers as the key manager, which would enable her to raise the necessary funds to buy the company at attractive rates.

But Sarah didn't want to pay extra for value she planned to create along the way. Satisfying this required her to fix the price of Bob's remaining 90 percent stake in PSI. Bob was sensitive to Sarah's concerns, but he was leery. What if the company added several new lines that doubled sales and profits? With a fixed option price, he wouldn't benefit from the increase in value. At the same time, he had grown tired of the game. He really needed to turn the company over to some fresh blood. It was invigorating to envision someone else having to argue with irate suppliers and customers. Maybe it was worth taking some risk to make that dream a reality.

As with most negotiations, this one boiled down to price and terms. At what price would Bob's 90 percent be fixed? And how long would Sarah have to exercise the option? Sarah proposed a price of $4 million for his stock and an option period of five years. Bob figured this put the price of PSI at just $4.5 million for the next five years ($4 million divided by 90%). Considering that he felt it was worth $6 to $7 million today, this wasn't aggressive enough to suit his needs. He countered at $5.2 million with an option period of 3 years. They ultimately settled on an option to buy at $5 million for four years. If Sarah was unable to exercise the option by then, her rights to buyout Bob would expire.

The option deal relied on a set of key operating considerations. Bob would deliver PSI with no interest-bearing debt at the time of the transfer or pay off any that remained from his proceeds from the buyout. Further, he would guarantee working capital (net current assets minus net current liabilities) of $1.5 million. Bob could distribute to himself cash over and above $1.5 million; likewise, he would have to put up cash of his own if working capital was less than $1.5 million. PSI would be required to spend at least as much on capital expenditures each year as its depreciation expense. Beyond that, Bob could take as much money from the business as he desired provided that doing so didn't violate any of the option covenants.

Sarah's lawyer advised her that she would need to pay Bob a consideration for the option to be legally enforceable. She pledged $20,000 for the right to buy Bob's shares.

The Bets

Bob and Sarah were each placing bets with this transaction. Bob wanted to plan his exit from PSI. He figured he would train Sarah for about 18 months and then turn most operations over to her. After the second year, he would assume the role of Chairman. Bob also figured that PSI's sales and profits would grow by about 10 percent per year, which would yield a recast EBITDA of about $1 million by the end of the fourth year. At that time, his equity would be worth $4.5 million (($1 million * 5) * 90%), so fixing his shares at $5 million did not scare him. He wasn't worried about the working capital provision, either. If anything, it would add to his pile. If Sarah wasn't able to buy his shares by the end of the option period, he would sell the company to an outsider.

Sarah had other ideas. She had studied PSI's market and operations carefully and she had a plan to grow the business faster than 10 percent a year. At that time, the repair and refurbishment segment represented only $1 million of the company's $8 million in sales. But it boasted gross margins of 45 percent compared to 21 percent for new pump sales. Sarah planned to market PSI's repair capabilities nationally, focusing mainly on other distributors of similar brands.

During her consulting career, Sarah had helped a company that distributed programmable logic controls formulate a national repair strategy. That company increased sales fivefold in a four year period. Sarah was convinced that she could duplicate this success at PSI. She believed that expanding the repair business would double the sales of the company in four years while tripling its profits.

Sarah projected that PSI would generate annual sales of $15 million by the end of the fourth year. More importantly, she expected EBITDA to rise to about $2 million. If that happened, 90 percent of PSI would be worth $9 million ($2 million * 5 * 90%). But according to the option agreement, she would have to pay only $5 million for Bob's shares! This was a classic arbitrage play, as Sarah could achieve a greater return from buying out PSI than the risk she was taking indicated.

After several months of negotiations, Sarah bought 10 percent of PSI. As Bob planned, she was running the company without a net midway through the second year. Her focus on the repair business clicked in the market, and PSI's sales and profits expanded rapidly. Three years after the buyin she exercised the option and acquired Bob's shares.

Bob was more than satisfied. Including Sarah's $350,000 buyin and $1.3 million in excess working capital he received at closing, he collected more than $6.6 million for his shares. In his mind, this confirmed his initial valuation of PSI.

Five years after the buyin, the business was worth $15 million. And everybody was happy.

BLUEPRINT

The Buyin – Buyout Game is a good strategy for those who want to hedge their bets when acquiring a business. Buyers reduce their risk by working in the company before betting the ranch. It's not even necessary for buyers to commit money up front, though most owners prefer they have a meaningful investment at stake.

Here are some key points to remember before attempting this Midas strategy:

1. Commitment is the name of the game. A full-time effort is required. It's nearly impossible to implement this strategy and work for a living at the same time.

2. Deal flow will be your lifeblood. Successful players generate multiple deal-looks each week. This requires the discipline to follow a strict process of contacting market players and evaluating opportunities.

3. Once the deal pipeline is open, be ready to filter candidates quickly, normally within an hour or two. The best way to do this is to post a list of five or six buyin criteria on your wall to serve as a constant reminder of your goals.

4. You have to multi-task. The tendency is to fall in love with one deal to the exclusion of all others. Tell your Board of Advisors that one of its jobs is to make sure this doesn't happen. It normally takes three to six months to complete a transaction. If marketing for new deals stops during the negotiating period, you might never get there.

5. Match your skill sets with your target company's needs to see if you can add value. This is an area where it's easy for buyers to kid themselves.

6. Successful players typically are minority owners from the outset. Owners are always viewed in a more positive light inside and outside of the company.

7. Negotiate all terms and agreements simultaneously. There is always some give-and-take in the process, which is an opportunity for buyers and sellers to learn whether they are suited to be partners.

8. To do a buyin, you need a smart growth plan for the business you're seeking to acquire. Just continuing to run the business as it has been operated probably won't create enough value to enable the eventual buyout. Further, the buyer needs to understand the company's capital alternatives well enough to know if a buyout can occur later.

9. It's important for the seller and buyer to agree on an arbitrator from the beginning. This person can be anyone that both sides respect. This is not binding arbitration; rather, this third party settles minor disputes before they fester into major brawls.

The first three to four months after the closing are usually rough on both sides of a buyin-buyout, but it's no time for either to second-guess the deal. Capitalism usually requires incredible doggedness as a rite of passage before success is granted. The Buyin – Buyout Game enables such a passage.

INVESTMENT BANKER MAN

On the day of closing, IB Man justifies
his exorbitant fee to opposing counsel

10

The Consolidation Math Game

AN ARBITRAGE STRATEGY

Tom Rudolph was down but not out. Aramco Packaging, the company of which he was the highly successful CEO, had just been sold to a behemoth in the packaging industry that wouldn't need his services any longer. At 45, Tom was out of a job for the first time in his adult life. But he wasn't exactly hurting. As CEO, he had earned a 2 percent stake in Aramco, which now represented almost $2 million in his favorite account, his own.

In six years at the helm, Tom had transformed Aramco from a sleepy little company doing about $20 million in annual sales to a vibrant middle market player ringing up more than $150 million each year. What's more, its pretax profits had surged from about $1 million per year to more than $20 million. And Tom had engineered this with almost no financial support from Aramco's owner. From the day Tom was hired the owner had shown more interest in taking money out of the business than putting it back in. And personal guarantees from the owner had not been a discussion topic for the entire time that Tom had been in charge. Even with these constraints, Tom had managed to create a tremendous amount of value in a fairly short period of time.

Now that he was on his own, could Tom duplicate that success? He had several things working in his favor. First, he had equity. He could squirrel away half of his Aramco stash for safe-keeping and still have $1 million to commit to an entrepreneurial effort. Second, he had experience. He knew the packaging industry well, having just spent 20 years making and selling just about every type of box. Third, he had developed a proven financial strategy. Tom knew exactly what to do: play the Consolidation Math Game.

Tom thought of the Consolidation Math Game as a real life version of Monopoly, except that there were no "Get Out of Jail Free" cards. Playing it required bold action. First, he would have to acquire a *platform company* in a segment of the packaging industry that he knew extremely well. Then he would acquire smaller *add-on companies* in the same segment that were suffering because they didn't have the critical mass to be competitive. Finally, he would absorb most of the general and administrative expenses from the add-on companies into the platform company. Freed from having to handle administrative chores, the owners of the acquired companies could return to what they loved most, selling. Tom formed a new entity, Corrugated Acquisition Company, LLC, and assembled a team of advisors comprising a corporate lawyer, a CPA, and an investment banker. The advisors would help him find a platform company to acquire and close the deal.

The Right Platform

Tom knew that not any platform company would do. His strategy required he find a company with a scalable business model, available systems and organization capacity, and managers who could handle hypergrowth. Because growth would occur via acquisitions, the managers also had to be adept at integrations. Tom's job was to find and negotiate the acquisitions and oversee the advisors as they raised the necessary capital. His plan would only be as good as his ability to capitalize it.

After several dry starts, Tom settled on trying to make All-American Packaging his platform company. All-American was a 10-year-old company owned by three fairly young managers who had started it after working together for an industry giant. There, they had taken a division through a period of hypergrowth but had ultimately felt stifled by the corporate culture. At All-American, each had responsibility for a critical functional area: administration, marketing and sales, or operations. They had positioned the company as a niche player that could command higher margins on its $40 million in annual sales than would normally be the case. Recast EBITDA totaled nearly $6 million and was expected to increase to roughly $7.5 million in the following year. Tom believed that the company's new state-of-the-art enterprise computer system would support a fivefold growth of the company.

After several months of negotiations, Corrugated Acquisition offered to buy 80 percent of All-American for $30 million. This put the enterprise value of All-American at $38 million, roughly six times its current EBITDA and five times projected EBITDA. The All-American managers kept 20 percent of the company as motivation to help Tom build his empire. The men signed a letter of intent, leaving Tom with only one problem: he was short $29 million.

A paradox of the private capital markets is that it's far easier to raise $30 million than it is to raise $3 million. Bankers and mezzanine lenders have a greater incentive to put up large amounts of money than small since larger companies tend to employ professional management teams with good control over the companies' operations. That decreases the risk of lending or investing. Tom knew that his deal was in that strike zone.

Tom's investment banker created a financing memorandum laying out Corrugated's strategy, plans, and capital requirements. The first stop was banks, which typically lend three to four times EBITDA for deals of his size. Tom secured a senior loan for $24 million. The banker told him that the interest rate, *LIBOR +200,* would be indexed to the London Interbank Offering Rate, the rate on dollar-denominated deposits traded between banks in London, plus 200 basis points or 2 percent. LIBOR is quoted for one month, three months, six months or one-year periods; Tom chose the six-month option, which meant his interest rate would reset every six months.

But that left Tom still $6 million short of his fundraising goal (he needed the extra million dollars to cover closing fees), so he turned to the mezzanine capital market. Tom learned that mezzanine sources will typically not lend more than two times a borrower's EBITDA. No problem, Tom thought. Even though he needed only $6 million, he decided to get a commitment for $12 million in case he needed more later. Between an 11 percent coupon rate and warrants that could be exercised for 5 percent of Corrugated's stock, Tom figured his all-in cost to access mezzanine was nearly 23 percent. The lender deferred repayment of the principal for two years, which would help Tom meet his cash flow projections.

The mezzanine provider explained that warrants help increase her yield. With a warrant, she would have a right to buy 5 percent of Corrugated Acquisition Company at a fixed price, also known as the exercise or strike price. Tom's mezzanine deal included *detachable* warrants, which meant the warrants could be repurchased by the borrower, starting in four years from the anniversary date of the investment at a pre-defined strike price. Tom negotiated a price of five times his company's EBITDA at the time of exercise times 5 percent. With an expected EBITDA of about $15 million in 4 years, Tom would have to pay the mezzanine source about $3.75 million for the warrants at the end of the fourth year (($15 million * 5) * 5%)), on top of the interest payments and repayment of the $6 million loan. Tom was concerned with the high cost of the mezzanine, but he knew that he couldn't close the deal without it.

Tom's *weighted cost of capital* was also fairly high. The bank loan, which carried an all-in cost of just 5 percent, accounted for 62 percent of his capital structure. But 23 percent was the equity held by Tom and the All-American managers, and they wanted returns of at least 35 percent on their investment. Some quick math showed the following:

Source of Funds	Amount	All-in Cost	Percent of Capital	Weighted Cost
Bank debt	$24,000,000	5%	62%	3.1%
Mezzanine	$6,000,000	23%	15%	3.5%
Equity	$9,000,000	35%	23%	8.1%
	$39,000,000		100%	15%

All told, Corrugated Acquisition Company's weighted cost of capital was about 15 percent – less than the mezzanine funds but significantly more than the bank financing. Tom knew that this was an important number: He would not begin creating value until Corrugated's return on capital exceeded it.

After months of messing around with lawyers, bankers and CPAs, Tom closed the deal. Now he could get back to playing the Consolidation Math Game.

Add-On Acquisitions

With his platform company in place, Tom immediately began to implement what he called a "buy left, sell right" strategy. He would not pay more than five times EBITDA for his add-on companies, which put him solidly on the left, or low end of the spectrum of acquisition multiples. But once they were integrated into his platform company, he hoped to sell the company for close to 10 times EBITDA, which would pay him on the right, or high end of the spectrum. The goal was an arbitraged return.

Market Segmentation by Sales and EBITDA Acquisition Multiples

Buy Left ←——————→ Sell Right

The first round of acquisition candidates all had one thing in common: they weren't creating value for their owners. Tom discovered that in his industry, the margins of companies with annual sales in the $5 to $10 million range had fallen to the point where owners could still earn a living but couldn't generate wealth. The following table summarizes an income statement for the first acquisition candidate – Simmons Inc.

Simmons Inc.

Revenue	$8,250,000
Gross Margin	23%
SG&A	1,350,000
EBITDA	$500,000

Jim Simmons had owned his namesake packaging company for 15 years. During the last five years his company's gross margins had fallen six points to 23 percent as its larger rivals had succeeded in implementing more efficient production processes. Jim wanted to keep working for at least five more years, but he knew that the company wouldn't be able to pay his $250,000 salary much longer. So when Tom called him to discuss selling Simmons to Corrugated, Jim was ready to listen.

With only $500,000 in profits, why was Tom interested in acquiring Simmons? There were two main reasons. First, Jim Simmons had a reputation as a great salesman; freeing him up to sell would add millions in annual sales. Second, almost all of the administrative costs that Simmons was incurring could be handled by All-American personnel, saving about $1 million per year.

But Tom still needed to figure out how much he was willing to pay for Simmons. A big part of the answer was found in Simmons's balance sheet:

Simmons Inc.
Summarized Balance Sheet

	20X3
Assets	
Accounts Receivable	$722,190
Inventory	450,057
Machinery & Equipment	955,123
Total Assets	$2,127,370
Liabilities	
Accounts Payable	531,578
Accrued Expenses	31,822
Long-term debt	450,000
Total Liabilities	1,013,400
Equity	1,113,970
Total Liabilities & Equity	$2,127,370

Tom would limit his offer to the amount he could borrow from the bank. After studying the balance sheet, calculating qualifying receivables and inventory, and reviewing an appraisal of the equipment, the bank agreed to $1.5 million. Tom wanted to lock Jim Simmons in for five years, so instead of offering him $1.5 million in cash, he offered $1 million plus a $500,000 seller note. The note would pay Jim 8 percent interest per year and would amortize over 5 years. Corrugated would also assume Simmons's $1 million in total debt and retain Jim to sell major accounts.

At first blush, it might seem expensive to spend $1.5 million and assume another $1 million in debt for a company with only $500,000 in annual earnings. But the deal accomplished several things for Tom. He added another $8 million in sales while saving about $1 million a year in G&A expenses. This meant he could expect a payback on his investment in about two years. He picked up an experienced national accounts salesperson, who Tom figured would sell an additional $3 to $5 million in packaging each year. And he did all this without using any cash.

As planned, Simmons was just the start. Tom eventually identified about 20 more acquisition candidates that fit his profile, buying six of them over the next 18 months. Including All-American's organic growth, Corrugated reached annual revenues of more than $100 million and EBITDA of more than $15 million within two years. Tom stayed aggressive in the third year, closing several more deals, but never paid more than five times EBITDA for an add-on company.

At the end of the fourth year, Tom sold Corrugated to one of its large competitors for $150 million cash and assumption of about $60 million in debt. That amounted to roughly 8.5 times EBITDA. Tom's partners – the All-American managers – received about $30 million from the sale, the second time in four years they had cashed a check for that amount. Tom netted nearly $100 million off his initial $1 million ante.

For Tom, playing the Consolidation Math Game was a lot like leveraging hotels on Boardwalk and Park Place. The main difference was that he wasn't just a player. In this game, he got to be the banker, too.

BLUEPRINT

The Consolidation Math Game aggressively grows business value by exploiting the market's tendency to pay higher acquisition multiples for larger companies. This strategy can be replicated in most industries by following some simple steps:

1. Make sure you're very knowledgeable about the segment in which the consolidation will occur. A seasoned manager will spot the right niches to exploit and is more likely to get buy-in from sources of capital and acquisition candidates.

2. Make sure that the market will pay more for larger companies in this segment. A few lunches with investment bankers familiar with the industry should clear this up.

3. This strategy requires ownership of a platform company with available systems and management capacity and key managers who are experienced in handling hypergrowth.

4. Study the industry to determine which companies aren't creating business value. This strategy works best where add-on companies can be identified and purchased within a fairly short period of time.

5. Add-on companies should be synergistic with the platform company and available at reasonable multiples (ideally less than five times EBITDA).

6. Contract with owners to keep them involved after you acquire their companies through the use of employment agreements, seller notes, earn-outs, or some combination of the three.

7. Don't fall in love with the consolidated result. Timing is important here. This strategy works best when initiated at the tail end of a recession and completed with a sale of the platform company within five years.

Buying left and selling right is not for the faint of heart. Success depends on having substantial experience in your industry, a strong team to help you raise capital and identify potential acquisitions, and the ability to integrate multiple companies into your platform. But if you've got the vision and courage to try, tremendous wealth might just await.

INVESTMENT BANKER MAN

Large retainers say the darndest things

The Midas Mentor

AN ARBITRAGE STRATEGY

Nick Womble was minding his own business one day when the phone rang. An old acquaintance of Nick's had given his phone number to a young entrepreneur in need of help. Now that young man was on the other end of the phone trying to sell Nick his business.

That young man was Ron Redstone. Ron owned and operated Recordation Services, Inc. (RSI), which provided accounting and financial services to government agencies under outsourcing contracts. Ron was a bright young entrepreneur in his mid-thirties who had started his business 12 years earlier and now wanted to sell it. He owned 100% of RSI and was a bona fide seller. He had established some wealth on paper, but what he really wanted was the liquidity to put a few bucks in the bank that would create lasting financial security for himself and his family. The only problem with this scenario, as is often the case with private business owners, was that Ron was trying to sell his company too early, and therefore, for too little.

Nick agreed to meet Ron and look over RSI's books. At the time, RSI had contracts with 10 agencies that were producing $5 million in revenue with recast earnings before interest, taxes, depreciation and amortization (EBITDA) of about $500,000. Ron hoped to sell the business for $2.5 million.

Nick was immediately impressed with this young, energetic business-man and his company. Ron was an expert in his field and passionate about his company. In his years of deal-making, Nick had kicked the tires of a lot of companies and he could see RSI's potential right away. It filled a vital civic and socially responsible role through its proprietary service programs; its business model had significant growth opportunities, low capital require-ments, and almost no inventory; and it had a durable advantage, no significant competition, and elastic pricing strategies. The result: recurring revenue and high net profits.

Nick agreed with Ron that RSI probably was worth $2.5 million, but there were no obvious takers. Strategic buyers wouldn't be interested be-cause of the company's uniqueness. It wouldn't fit cleanly into an existing corporate entity, which meant a buyer wouldn't benefit from any synergies. It wouldn't be attractive to private investors because there weren't enough assets to leverage. And although it was a cash cow, RSI was reliant on a small number of customers and in a single geographic area, a risk factor that would put off cash flow lenders. Even if these obstacles hadn't existed, the deal would be too small to interest private equity investors.

Nick had a better idea. He suggested that instead of doing a buyout, he would do a buyin; that is, he would become Ron's partner. Nick did not want to go to work everyday but he did love to mentor young businesspeople, (something he had done in nearly 90 prior deals), and he badly wanted to stay in the business game. Ron wanted to create some real wealth for him-self, but he didn't know how to take the company to the next level. If a sale wasn't going to happen now, Ron wanted RSI to generate enough cash flow to satisfy his short-term financial needs via some sizable distributions, and within the next five years, he wanted to sell the business for at least $10 million, which would satisfy his long-term financial needs.

So Nick and Ron made a deal – coach and quarterback, teacher and student, Socrates and Plato all over again. In other words, Nick would be Ron's Midas Mentor.

Payday

As they hoped, Nick's Midas touch and Ron's entrepreneurial passion proved an excellent match. A little over four years after their relationship had started, they sold RSI. All of Ron's goals were realized: The business had flourished, growing from 10 contracts to nearly 100; revenues had increased from $5 million to $25 million and recast EBITDA had increased from $500,000 to just over $5 million; and Ron received more than $5 million in total distributions during that time (twice his original asking price for RSI) and nearly $20 million upon selling the business (eight times his original asking price).

Now the obvious question: "How did all of this happen? How in the world do you increase a company's worth by a factor of 12 simply by including a Midas Mentor?"

Nick helped Ron create value in several distinct ways. First, he retooled RSI's business model to generate recurring sales and scalable operations. Second, he gave Ron access to value-adding external resources. Third, he helped Ron increase his value to the company by putting him on a path toward self-improvement. Last but certainly not least, Nick helped Ron execute a wealth-maximizing exit.

The first contribution Nick made was to help Ron develop a five-year strategic plan. This led directly to the decision to concentrate resources on one area of the business to quickly increase RSI's penetration in the industry. The focus they chose turned out to be a perfect place to start because it offered exclusive contracts, little competition, and, thus, higher sustainable margins. RSI would leverage its success with existing agencies to sign up new clients for this initial program – and then later go back and offer other programs with similar characteristics to its entire customer base.

Next, Nick introduced Ron and RSI to a number of value-adding resources. First, he recommended a national accounting firm to create some financial transparency in the company and start the annual audit process. Up to that point, RSI produced only yearly accounting compilations, which were not particularly useful for outside investors. Nick also recommended a well-known law firm. RSI had been engaged in several lawsuits over the years, which was not unusual for its industry. The new law firm's substantial contacts, experience and savvy mitigated one of the risks of owning the company.

Third, Nick helped make Ron a more well-rounded person, both personally and professionally. With 40-plus years in business and deal-making, Nick was an ideal sounding board for Ron's ideas. He also gave Ron access to his extensive network of connections. In the rare times that Nick had not experienced a situation himself, he usually knew someone who had and brought that individual into the fold. Nick also increased Ron's circle of influence. He introduced Ron to the Board of Directors of a major medical research institute, which later gave Ron's daughter a research grant. Nick also sponsored Ron for induction into the Young President's Organization, where he met other successful owners and executives and gained an avenue for professional association and distinction. Nick also encouraged Ron to enroll in an MBA Program at a local university. Through these efforts, Nick had helped Ron expand and elevate his network and add new skill sets, helping him personally and contributing to the strategic plan the two men had for the business.

Finally, Nick orchestrated and then shepherded the exit event. He put together a top-notch team of professionals, including a transaction lawyer with whom Nick had done all of his prior deals. Nick also found an investment bank with relevant industry experience to run an auction process that created value on its own. And he led the negotiations for RSI. He set up parameters with the entire deal team: Everyone had a say, and very few discussions happened without the bulk of the selling team present.

Once the transaction was complete, Nick ensured that RSI had transition management in place. When Ron decided not to stay with the company, Nick initiated a search for a new President and CEO, who, once hired, quickly added value. When he learned that the COO/CFO also planned to leave, Nick found a temporary replacement for the six-month transition period to put the buyer at ease and keep the deal moving forward.

If any of this sounds simple, it wasn't. Without Nick, Ron would have quickly gotten in over his head. It was absolutely essential for Ron to have a Midas Mentor guide him to a wealth-creating conclusion. Because, as Nick is so fond of saying, "No one can see their own backswing."

BLUEPRINT

Most business owners would benefit from a Midas Mentor. These coaches with the golden touch have already demonstrated the ability to create corporate wealth. They are Midas Managers who have decided to give something back to the system. Midas Mentors are not merely consultants, however. The following table shows some key differences between the two callings:

	Midas Mentor	**Consultant**
Business experience	Broad	Narrow
Expertise	Strategic	Tactical
Ultimate goal	Create wealth	Solve a problem
Fee structure	Typically tied to a percentage of wealth created	Typically by the hour, not based on success

The most important difference between a consultant and a Midas Mentor is their reason for being. Consultants exist to solve problems. Midas Mentors exist to create wealth. That distinction influences how each is compensated. Consultants get paid by the hour or by the project. Midas Mentors get paid a portion of the wealth they have helped to create.

Perhaps this story will help illustrate the difference between the roles various advisors play. A business owner is walking down the street when all of a sudden, the sidewalk gives way. The owner finds himself in a hole that is 50 feet deep and no way out. As luck would have it, the owner's CPA happens to walk by. The owner screams at the CPA to get him out. The CPA gets busy on the task at hand, and after about an hour, floats down a piece of paper to the owner. On it is a detailed explanation of the accident. Although an excellent history of the event, it does nothing to solve the problem.

Next, the owner's consultant shows up. "Get me out of here," the owner yells. Pleasant and helpful as always, the consultant gets to work. After two more hours, another piece of paper floats down, this one with a detailed draw-ing of a ladder, but no tools or materials with which to build it.

Finally, a Midas Mentor wanders by. "Are you OK?" he yells down. The owner is just starting to recount the farcical events of the past few hours when the Midas Mentor interrupts him to tell him to move to one side of the hole. Then he jumps into the hole with him. Beside himself, the owner shrieks that now they are both stuck in this awful predicament. Hearing this, the Midas Mentor puts his hand on the owner's shoulder to reassure him. "It will be OK," he says. "I've been here before."

Most business owners are stuck in a hole of their own and are receiving little, if any, help getting out. They need a Midas Mentor. But Midas Mentorship succeeds only if the business owner has the following character-istics: a strong desire to grow their wealth (to get out of the hole); a belief in the ability of the Midas Mentor to help them do that; an open mind and willingness to *listen* to the Midas Mentor; and courage — personally and in the business — to proceed in a bold fashion.

The strategies RSI implemented during Nick's tenure didn't just help Ron sell the business years later — they made it possible. Without them, the company might not have been sold or if it had, likely wouldn't have fetched such a high price.

Indeed, even without a sale, the actions that Nick encouraged Ron to take with RSI helped it to prosper at the same time it was evolving into a very salable business. Quite often, business owners don't contemplate selling their company until it is too late. Midas Managers always run their companies in a manner that will make a sale possible, regardless of if they plan to sell or not. They know that a company should always have an exit strategy in place. It might change over time, but it better be there.

Remember the old adage, "It's not what you know, it's who you know? Midas Mentors know how true it is. Thus, one of Nick's most important jobs was introducing Ron and RSI to value-creating contacts. Several of these were unknown to Nick, identified by other contacts as the best possible resource. Nick didn't know everyone, but if he made a few calls, he could get the Pope on the line.

Here again, on his own, Ron could never have assembled the deal team that his Midas Mentor did. He probably wouldn't have known even where to start, since his local contacts likely wouldn't know how to access the national-caliber players he needed. Even if Ron had been able to reach the right people, he likely couldn't have gotten them to play ball with him. Midas Mentors add value by knowing and understanding the deal process and the caliber of player it takes to get a good deal done.

So how do you find your Midas Mentor? The following steps will help attract the right person:

1. Ask for Help: The Midas Mentorship process starts when a business owner realizes he or she must do something differently to achieve his or her goals. This is often the most difficult step because it involves honesty, humility, and proactivity.

2. Find the Right Person: Midas Mentors are a rare breed and thus not easy to spot. Not just any retired businessperson will do. Midas Mentors are typically already independently wealthy so their motives go beyond mere financial gain. Coaching helps them stay young, keeps them in the game, and makes them feel needed.

3. Share the Wealth: Mentors are not totally altruistic. They typically receive a monthly retainer to insure the owner is serious about receiving their advice (people who pay nothing for advice usually treat it as worthless). Then Mentors receive some percentage of the wealth that they help create. If a company is worth $5 million when the Mentor arrives and $25 million when it is sold, the Mentor gets a percentage of the

difference, typically 20 percent or more. While this might seem extravagant, consider that the owner makes an additional $16 million because of the Midas help (($25 million - $5 million) multiplied by 80%). With RSI, Ron Redstone increased his net worth by more than $25 million, in large part because of his involvement with Nick Womble.

Midas Mentoring is an arbitrage strategy because it enables a business owner to increase returns dramatically without taking on any more risk. And if the owner is lucky, the Midas Mentor will become a teacher, partner, and friend for life.

Part III

BUSINESS MODELS

I2

Business Models IOI

The Conceptual Age is all about business models. A business model describes how an owner organizes a company, its strategy, and its tactics to meet his or her goals. In an always-on globalized economy, business models have become vitally important because the main constraint on creating wealth is an owner's imagination.

Traditional business models are based on a command-and-control structure. Every step in the process chain is owned and tightly managed. This has led to corporations that are over-structured, over-controlled, and over-managed. In other words, an MBA's dream! Conceptual business models distribute most of the key missions and key functions to entities outside of the company. Instead of building dams that stymie the flow of intellectual capital, conceptual business models give people canoes and compasses to allow them to navigate it. Paradoxically, less control generates more output.

Conceptual business models are built upon networks of strategically involved citizens who can act quickly and collaboratively to address niches. Owning your intellectual capital and outsourcing everything else is the ultimate Conceptual Age business model. This idea rubs many business owners the wrong way – especially those over 60 years old. These graybeards are control freaks bred in the Information Age, when anything the least bit pro-prietary was locked away in a vault inaccessible to even employees.

In the Conceptual Age, change is occurring geometrically and keeping up requires a different mindset. The gigantic global economy encourages and rewards small organizations. D eveloping virtual communities of part-ners and consumers is now the main activity for an owner . The next six chapters describe Midas Managers who had the foresight to understand this and implement conceptual business models in their companies.

Chapter 13: Design and Deliver

Designing a product or service and then delivering it quickly and economi-cally is a hallmark activity of the Conceptual Age. This chapter demonstrates how, simply by outsourcing steps in a process chain that don't create value and leveraging and maximizing intellectual capital, a company can blow away historical financial metrics. The Midas Manager in this chapter used this strategy to generate $2.5 million in sales and more than $500,000 in profits — per employee!

Chapter 14: The Nature of Niches

Globalization grants niches to those who can spot them. Instead of trying to compete intergalactically, small to mid-sized company owners need to be-come niche-aholics. That means identifying the intellectual capital in their companies and matching it up with niches that leverage this know-how. There's never any shame in establishing niches with $1 to $2 million in annual sales, especially if all it takes is maximizing capabilities you already have. The Midas Manager in this chapter created a small empire that way.

Chapter 15: The Day Brazil Called

In a virulently capitalistic global economy, every small company is just one phone call away from oblivion. Mid-sized companies might get two. The Midas Manager in this chapter received such a phone call from Brazil, in which h e learned the downside to participating in the world's largest contiguous market: everyone dumps their stuff in the U.S. The issue is not whether your markets will be attacked; rather, it's what you'll do about it when they are. The proper response might be to come up with a completely different business model.

Chapter 16: Productize or Die!

Most project engineering, contracting, and service companies are constantly reinventing the wheel, treating every new job in a one-off manner. The company profiled in this story was no different: Engineers waited for the phone to ring and started each project from scratch, sort of like old-fashioned cooking. But the Midas Manager in this chapter proved that anything a company does can be productized in the Conceptual Age.

Chapter 17: Push or Pull?

American companies have historically pushed their products and services onto the market and sent their marketing departments out to pick off as many customers as possible. Now it makes more sense to let products and services be pulled into a market. This chapter illustrates how to reconceptualize a traditional business model to take advantage of open source dynamics.

Chapter 18: The Instant Company

It used to take generations to create substantial wealth; now, two or three years will do, thanks to instant companies. An instant company starts with a conceptual business model. It launches a "hit" product or service like a rocket, outsourcing a lmost every process step by leveraging — but not owning — worldwide capabilities. The Midas Manager in this chapter implemented just such a model and found out how quickly the Conceptual Age creates wealth.

In business today, operational excellence isn't enough. Focus on shaving a few pennies off your costs and you'll wind up being scalped by your competition. What's required now is the right-brained creativity to design imaginative new business models that can deliver nuclear impact in the marketplace. Sometimes a manager needs to be on the other side of the looking glass to do that. Welcome to the Conceptual Age!

I3

Design and Deliver
A BUSINESS MODEL STRATEGY

As owner of Cosmetic Components Corp., Scott Livingston was living a jet-setting lifestyle. Summer was only a month old and he had just returned from his sixth overseas trip of the year. Scott didn't particularly enjoy all of that business travel, but the innovative business model he had implemented depended on him spanning the globe for wealth-creating opportunities.

Scott had founded the company 10 years prior to supply parts to the U.S. beauty industry – items such as lipstick tubes and compact cases. Scott knew this industry well. In his previous life as an executive at a large multinational cosmetics company, he had been indoctrinated in the integrated American business model, which called for owning every step of the process chain. Consequently, Scott knew a good deal about manufacturing as well as selling these products.

The Cosmetics Industry

There were a handful of well-known international cosmetics companies at the time, and Scott had worked for one of the most famous. The industry grew from the turmoil of the 1960s, the decade that launched women into the professional work force. By the mid-1970s, the burgeoning beauty industry

had convinced women of all ages that cover girl looks were not only possible, they were required.

As a result, the serious players in the industry adopted integrated process
chains. This meant they owned every step of the process for manufacturing
and distributing their products. They outsourced advertising to Madison Avenue and final sales to retailers like Macy's and Bloomingdales, but in between,
they owned every step.

After graduating from college, Scott had entered into a management training program at the company to learn the cosmetics business. He spent a couple
of years at the plants, then a few years in marketing, and finally did a stint in
the international division. Many of the industry's factories were overseas, so
Scott traveled extensively, giving him a global view of the business and loads
of contacts. Both would serve him well when he quit the big company to start
Cosmetic Components.

Although he possessed a wealth of knowledge about the industry, Scott
had only $100,000 to invest in his startup, and most of this was borrowed.
But Scott hadn't chosen to leave the big company; he had followed the Siren
Song of business ownership. He had to control his destiny, and the possibility of failure wasn't going to deter him.

Scott's limited funds meant that he needed to re-invent the wheel. He
certainly couldn't afford to build million-dollar factories. He needed a new
business model.

Design and Deliver

Scott dubbed his new business model "Design and Deliver." His new company would design parts for beauty products, outsource the manufacturing,
and then deliver finished products to customers. This model solved his prob-

lem of factory investment and meant he could leverage his intellectual capital, that is, his knowledge of the industry and long list of contacts, to support his efforts. Here are a few ways Scott could put his know-how and network to use:

- He knew how to manufacture parts for the beauty industry on a worldwide stage
- He knew how to build a design and marketing staff that could get the attention of major cosmetics companies
- He knew already most of the manufacturers because they supplied his previous employer (or wanted to)
- He knew how to get salespeople to produce and listen to customers to get feedback for the design and marketing staff

Scott's intellectual capital, the sum of all of his skill sets, contacts and experience, would turn out to be far more important to the success of Cosmetic Components than mere money. Almost anyone can raise money, but few could convert intellectual capital into a cash flow machine.

Design and Marketing

Scott's first two hires were the most important he would ever make. Cosmetic Components needed sales. Because of his contacts, Scott knew he could generate about $2.5 million in sales himself, but he needed at least twice that to reach his financial targets in the first year. He found it in Bill Masters, a veteran of the cosmetics industry who, like Scott, had apprenticed in most areas of the business. Also like Scott, he had tired of big-company politics.

Bill would need direction, but he had a somewhat captive customer base generating $2 million in annual sales and a good shot at getting the same amount in new business. Scott gave Bill a salary of $75,000 plus 20 percent of profits above a gross margin of 25 percent. Thus, if Bill was able to sell $5 million in components with gross margins of 30 percent, he would earn a $50,000 bonus ($5 million times ((30% - 25%) * 20%))). Star salespeople could sell $10 million in beauty components per year, and by his third year, Bill had done just that.

Scott next hired a young but experienced designer who had worked for him at the big company. This person was a guru in compact case design, where Cosmetic Components would initially make its name. She received a salary of $75,000 and 1 percent of sales of each new component sold. Within three years, Cosmetic Components was selling more than $10 million worth of products that qualified for the bonus. Every year Scott added a design guru in another area of packaging, always using the same incentive plan.

Within five years of its founding, Cosmetic Components employed eight salespeople who averaged $6 million apiece in annual sales and $100,000 in pay. The company also employed five design gurus and a handful of administrative personnel. Total sales exceeded $50 million, with pretax profits of almost $10 million — a lot for a company that didn't run a single factory and had fewer than 20 people on the payroll.

Manufacturing

What accounted for this success? For one thing, Scott didn't just outsource. He *partnered*. Offshore factories were recruited to supply 100 percent of Cosmetic Components' need in a particular product area. For example, all of Scott's compacts and jars came from one company in China, all extruded tubes were produced by one company in Mexico, and all lipstick cases were made a company in Thailand. Scott negotiated exclusive supply agreements that prohibited his partners from supplying parts to his competition and prevented them from selling directly to consumers. The company received shipments in leased space in public warehouses and then broke them apart for customers, shielding the customer from the manufacturer.

This manufacturing arrangement solved several problems for Scott. First, it eliminated the need for him to invest in manufacturing, which made his model both low-cost and scalable. Second, Scott's partners were extremely capable of producing the required parts, so he didn't have to worry about supply disruptions. Third, Cosmetic Components was usually the largest or second-largest customer for a partner so it got rapid responses anytime there was a problem. Scott could even call the owner. Fourth, with geographic diversity, Cosmetic Components was not overly exposed to fluctuations in weather or currency.

Scott's designers worked with each partner to help prepare them for future business. In the case of compacts, the partner needed to invest about $500,000 in new injection molds each year. As long as it received Cosmetic Components' molding business, it would cover that cost. Of course, the cost of the mold typically ended up baked into the piece price, but Scott was still better off, because he didn't tie up cash in the process. In fact, Cosmetic Components was able to save hundreds of thousands of dollars each year simply managing the float between payment from its customers (within 45 days of delivery) and payment to its partners (75 days after receiving a shipment).

Delivery

Cosmetic Components was solely responsible for delivering its products to customers. This was important for several reasons. First, it served as a check on quality and shipping. Scott took great pride in these areas, and when there was a problem, one of his sales coordinators reacted quickly. Sales coordinators supported salespeople and were responsible for following up with customers after each shipment. Adding a step in the process chain gave the company a chance to monitor its performance while helping it forge a deeper connection with customers. As time went by, many new ideas emanated from those conversations.

Cosmetic Components had nearly all of its products made to order. This enabled it to operate a $50 million business with less than $500,000 of inventory. Only a small amount was kept just in case a customer got into trouble. Delivery of products automatically triggered the company's computers to generate re-order messages or emails to salespeople for follow-up with customers.

The Beauty of a Scalable Model

The best attribute of Scott's design and deliver business model was that it was scalable. Cosmetic Components could add $10 to $20 million in sales with just a handful of new hires. And every time Scott noticed a new area of cosmetics that he wanted to enter, he could follow the same script:

- Hire a salesperson with an existing customer base and pay him or her aggressively
- If the market potential is large enough, hire a dedicated design guru and offer him or her some upside

- Partner with a qualified and motivated offshore manufacturer (sometimes an existing partner) to handle 100 percent of production for that item
- Deliver to customer and follow up to determine if needs were met and generate ideas for future products

Scott's model was scalable because it leveraged intellectual capital, not machines or financial capital. As he realized early on, intellectual capital, while intangible, is far more important to an owner creating wealth than the old-fashioned forms of capital. In just a few short years, Cosmetic Components' business model had created a wonderful lifestyle for its employees and substantial wealth for its owner.

BLUEPRINT

Globalization is leading many American business owners to adopt design and deliver business models, which are subsets of conceptual business models. Implementers of these models literally think their way to a goal. Intellectual capital is their main asset, and it can be quite productive. In the case of Cosmetic Components, average sales per employee exceed $2.5 million a year.

Design and deliver models are paradoxical, in that they do more with less. Of course, this is counterintuitive for most businesspeople, who are accustomed to owning every step of the process chain. Let's face it: most business owners want to control every aspect of their business. Successful outsourcing requires not only a different mindset, but also development of skill sets that are different from those needed to own each step of the chain. It can be difficult to even decide what steps to outsource. For example, should the selling function be owned or outsourced? How does an owner make this decision? How does an owner decide which steps to outsource? What is intellectual capital? Let's try to answer these questions.

Every company has a process chain, which comprises the steps required to provide a product or service to the customer. Many companies employ a fairly long process chain, with 10 steps or more. Consider the steps that investment bankers follow to raise private equity capital:

1. The firm markets its services
2. The firm meets a prospective client and learns its needs
3. An engagement letter proposal is forwarded to the prospective client
4. After some negotiations, the prospective client signs the engagement letter

5. The firm creates a memorandum that tells the client's story and describes how it plans to use the capital

6. The firm researches appropriate private equity sources

7. The memorandum is sent to potential investors

8. Investors with an interest in the deal meet the client

9. Investors with a further interest provide a term sheet

10. The parties negotiate

11. A term sheet is signed

12. Lawyers draft legal documents

13. The client closes on the funding

The first 11 steps describe the investment banker's process chain; steps 12 and 13 are for a closing attorney.

Now, suppose an investment banker wants to implement a design and deliver business model. What steps will be owned versus outsourced? In order to decide this, the investment banker must first identify the firm's *intellectual capital*. Every business with a place in the market has unique capabilities that it can leverage to create value. This is its intellectual capital, or know-how. The more intellectual capital a company possesses, the more value it can create for its customers and thereby create wealth for itself. This is what is meant by a *positive value proposition*.

Most successful investment banking firms are good at marketing and attracting clients and negotiating a deal to a close. Thus, the firm should always own steps one through four and step 10. The other steps, such as researching sources of equity and preparing the memorandum, it should outsource, since there are firms that specialize in these areas and supply quality products more cheaply than the investment banking firm can. As a general rule, steps that don't create value should be undertaken within a company (not outsourced) only when: a) no outside vendor is available; b) the cost of outsourcing is prohibitive; or c) confidentiality forbids it.

So how does a manager decide which process steps to own as opposed to outsource? Steps that rely on unique capabilities (intellectual capital) are owned; everything else is outsourced. A company's ability to uniquely perform a step in its process chain is what creates wealth. This position leverages intellectual capital and the necessary steps should be owned by the company. Non value-adding steps should be outsourced, but controlled. Controlling a step allows you to exert tremendous influence over its completion without the risk or cost of owning the resource that does the job. The company that chooses to outsource loses some control over the step's completion. The difference can be understood by supposing a company is considering the most effective method of organizing its sales effort. The company can: a) own the sales team, by directly employing each salesperson; b) control the sales team, by contracting with independent sales representatives; or c) outsource sales to distributors. Depending on the company's goals, any of these actions may make sense.

The benefits of outsourcing are simple: It lets a company dedicate more time and resources to value-creating activities. Outsourcing also helps a company leverage its unique capabilities. This is the foundation beneath conceptual business models. In the Conceptual Age, thinking one's way to a solution is not only mandatory – it can also be wealth-creating.

14

The Nature of Niches

A BUSINESS MODEL STRATEGY

By all appearances, Jack Ripley was a regular guy. He drove an ordinary car, lived in the same modest house for 20 years, and never drew much attention to himself.

Jack's business, Screw Machine Products (SMP), was rather ordinary, too. Housed in a nondescript building in the industrial part of town, it made a variety of small metal parts from old Brown & Sharpe screw machines – also known as Brownies. For year's, his wife had worked alongside, supporting his entrepreneurial dreams, and now his daughter had joined the business. His employees had been with him for a couple of decades, long enough to become Jack's surrogate family. In other words, he was a typical owner of a typical American company.

But Jack had a secret he kept from most of the world: He was a *niche-aholic*. Jack's addiction to niches helped SMP to earn several million dollars each year.

Of course, this had not always been the case. Jack's first decade in business had taught him that hard work alone wasn't enough to create wealth. Just about everyone worked hard, especially in his industry. The mantra was "sell it for less and make it up on volume," and SMP did just that. But one day Jack confessed to his wife that he was tired of spending 70 percent of his day on the shop floor, running from one machine to another that required his attention, and never getting ahead.

His frustration came to a boiling point when Jack thoroughly analyzed SMP's invoices one month. About 60 percent of his business was generating gross margins of less than 21 percent. These sales represented SMP's "commodity" products. Jack realized that there was not enough volume in the world to make up for such low margins. When he applied overhead expenses dedicated to this business, it was clear to Jack that he was riding a loser.

Jack decided to focus on two things: raising prices for the 60 percent of his business that was underperforming and studying the 40 percent of the business that had higher margins, SMP's specialty products.

The strategy for the former was simple. Jack jacked up prices on every commodity part until they were all generating gross margins of 35 percent. About one-third of his customers balked and found a cheaper supplier. The rest, who represented almost $1.5 million in annual sales, were now generating a return that Jack thought would create value. The following table verified his suspicions:

Screw Machine Products

Commodity Profitability Analysis – Before/After Price Increase

	Before Price Increase	After Price Increase
Revenues	$2,000,000	$1,500,000
Gross Profit %	21%	35%
Overhead Expenses*	450,000	400,000
Pretax Profits	$(30,000)	$125,000

*Overhead expenses decreased after the price increase due to savings realized from lower sales.

The more interesting challenge was improving the part of his business that was already very profitable. Specialty product sales also totaled about $1.5 million a year. Comprised of two product lines, specialty products were made of exotic materials, such as titanium and monel. One product, called Gauge Saver, was launched about six years before for the Navy. Submarines have lots of gauges, and Jack had created a valve that attached to gauges that prevented fluid and air spikes. There wasn't a tremendous demand for this valve, but every submarine needed one, and SMP sold about $750,000 worth every year.

The other specialty product was a metal housing used in a variety of health care applications. These small "critical medical housings" were made from titanium, a very difficult metal to machine, but over the years, SMP had become known for its skill at doing just that. Purely through word of mouth, this business had grown to about $750,000 in annual revenues itself.

While these specialty businesses represented half of SMPs sales, they were responsible for most of its profits, boasting 60 percent gross margins. Jack constructed the following income statement:

Screw Machine Products
Specialty Products

Revenues	$1,500,000
Gross Profit %	60%
Overhead Expenses	400,000
Pretax Profits	$500,000

Despite their profitability, both specialty businesses had been running on auto-pilot. SMP built them without any organized marketing effort and was dedicating few resources toward maintaining their revenues. But both products were sold into markets that were large enough to support increased sales. Jack believed each could double in size without attracting the attention of competitors.

All of this got Jack thinking even bigger. What if he re-oriented SMP toward producing only specialty products? In other words, what if SMP focused entirely on niches? It seemed almost counter-intuitive to Jack, but he liked it anyway. So he took an inventory of SMP's core competencies:

Screw Machine Products
Core Competencies

1. Precise machining of exotic metals
2. World class quality control and reporting systems
3. Profitable producer of short runs
4. An owner with a talent for spotting, funding, and exploiting niches

SMP had years of experience machining exotic metals, such that it now was a competitive advantage. Since the company provided work to the Navy and to the health care system, it had a state-of-the-art quality control system with critical certifications. Because Brownies were old and out of style, Jack had acquired several dozen of them inexpensively, and this gave SMP the ability to leave numerous machines set up and ready for production, eliminating costs and making short runs profitable. Finally, Jack himself was a core competency. He had developed the ability to spot niche opportunities and the patience and persistence to exploit them.

Jack devised a novel way to think of a niche-centric business model. He likened it to the branches hanging off a tree:

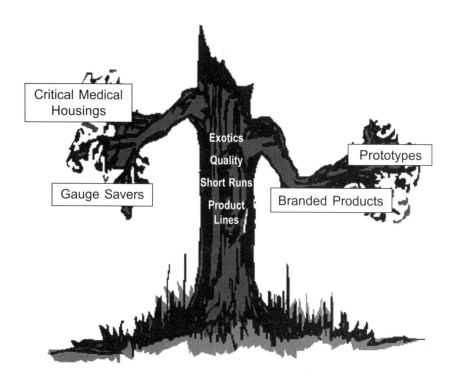

This observation changed Jack's life. He was now a man on a mission: Establish at least five niches for SMP to attack, with one or two more constantly under development. Jack was a realist, so he figured that even the best niche would eventually get competitors' attention. He needed to be constantly on the lookout for new ones.

It quickly became clear to Jack that his role in his company needed to change. Instead of relief operating or loading trucks, he needed to focus on market opportunities. He started slowly, dedicating one day each week to meeting with customers and analyzing what they told him. Most niches emanate from listening to customers complain about their problems and then determining how to make a market out of the solution. Jack discovered that "dry wells" were more plentiful than he had hoped, but nobody said it would be easy making a fortune.

Once Jack got into the swing of niche-making, he needed to organize the process. Visiting customers eventually required two or three days a week. The issue was not so much discovering opportunities as it was identifying promising niches. Jack had learned long before that the market would let you work for free or at least for little return. So he put on paper criteria that would help him determine if an opportunity could be converted into a niche:

1. Can the product or service hang easily from SMP's intellectual capital tree?

2. Is the niche defensible and sustainable?

3. Does the product or service have the potential for at least $750,000 in annual sales within three years?

4. Does the product or service promise gross margins of at least 45 percent?

5. If the product or service requires a capital investment, will the payback come in less than three years?

Jack had this list on his office wall, not far from a sign that read, "Gone Niching." Whenever he was away, even on vacation, he would hang the sign on his door. The phrase eventually became part of the company's culture. Employees liked the idea that the owner was always looking out for their futures.

Even though Jack only took on projects if he felt they would ultimately lead to a niche, he had to traverse a difficult learning curve. But as with any new skill set, Jack got better at listening to the market and identifying possibilities. He also learned discipline. Rather than taking whatever work came over the transom, Jack now turned down 80 percent of the opportunities he uncovered, using his list of criteria to help him focus.

Jack went after low-hanging fruit first; or, to use another fruit metaphor, he made lemonade when others could only see lemons. For many years SMP had specialized on short-run, low-volume machining, just the sort of business that everyone else in the industry despised. Most of SMP's competitors would take the low-volume stuff only as part of a package that included higher-volume runs. So Jack went to a couple of industry shows and offered to partner with the competition. SMP would take runs of less than a 1,000 pieces and they would get the rest. Within two months, 10 different competitors had signed up to send their low-volume orders to SMP and 10 more had included it in their bids for new business. SMP quickly became the industry's short-run source with more than $1 million in annual sales and 45 percent gross margins.

In his quest for niches, Jack also dabbled in acquisitions. He put out the word to business brokers that he was interested in product lines he could move into his plant. The only constraints: the products needed to be manufactured on screw machines and sport annual sales of more than $750,000. It took about six months of prospecting, but Jack eventually got such an opportunity. The products, PR Valves, (for "pressure relief") were used to release built-up pressure in fire extinguishers and other containers. Although the line generated only $1 million in annual sales, it fit SMP's profile perfectly. All of the selling company's revenues came from PR Valves, so all of its fixed and variable expenses were applied against sales. Since SMP already had a book of business that absorbed most of its costs, it only had to allocate a small portion of the total overhead plus direct costs to the product line, rendering it a much more profitable business.

The following shows the product line profitability before and after the acquisition:

PR Valves
Profitability Before/After Acquisition

	Before Acquisition	After Acquisition
Revenues	$1,000,000	$1,000,000
Gross Profit %	45%	45%
Overhead Expenses	550,000	200,000
Pretax Profits	$(100,000)	$250,000

Jack acquired the PR Valve line for $200,000, allowing him to beat his payback goal by two years. He also was able to dedicate $75,000 a year in marketing costs to help the business grow, something the prior owner never did.

After five to six years of niching, Jack had built SMP into a company with $8.5 million in annual sales and pretax profits of more than $2 million. On top of the earnings, he received a $600,000 salary and his wife and daughter each took out $150,000 annually. All of this was accomplished on the backs of six fairly small niches. Although Jack was having too much fun to consider selling SMP, he took comfort in the knowledge that it would fetch $12 to $14 million if he ever changed his mind.

BLUEPRINT

There are numerous ways to define "niching." It can be meeting an unmet customer need, filling a hole in the market, or providing a product or service that is defensible, sustainable, and delivers a return greater than the underlying risk. Since I created this last definition, it is my favorite.

Most Midas Managers spend large amounts of their time looking for niches, causing some people to wonder if they work at all. But Midas Managers don't work in the conventional sense. While most company owners view business as the equivalent of playing checkers, a tactical and linear game, our heroes view it as a game of chess, where strategy is what decides the winner. Since strategies and niches are not typically hatched in the office, Midas Managers spend only one or two days a week there. Put another way, paid managers manage the business, but Midas Managers create wealth.

Like chess, niching is a difficult game to play well. Wealth is created by understanding what the market needs and is willing to pay for, and that understanding doesn't come cheap or easy. It doesn't hurt to have a wildcatter's taste for risk, too. One Midas Manager told me that she knew she was on the right track trying to create a new market when her key managers all said it would never work. Of course, most people couldn't see a niche even if it were right in front of their nose, but repeatedly pitching them to her team gave her a chance to develop the story. As soon as she truly believed her own pitch she committed resources to move ahead.

Globalization has dramatically affected the size of niches. During the 1980's a middle market company could develop a niche with $50 million per year in sales and defend it. Then, in the 1990s, the sandbox got bigger and the size of niches fell in half, to about $25 million. This halving has happened again in the current decade. Today, if a mid-sized company gets much above $10 million in sales from a niche, the world shows up, and they're not looking to buy.

This is why most successful middle market companies are really amalgams of niches hanging from an intellectual capital tree. We might call these companies *niched conglomerates*. Successful companies often operate in six to eight niches, each with less than $10 million in sales but tremendous overall profitability. For Midas Managers, it's not about total sales; it's about how much wealth is created – now and in the future.

The following steps can be used to replicate Jack's niching strategy:

1. Understand your costs before playing the niche game. Gross profit margin, as used in this story, means accounting for the direct material, direct labor, and allocated overhead for a particular product. Most small companies do not know the true gross margin of their products or services. In other words, they don't know where they make money. Updating inadequate financial systems can tell you just that and is thus a good place to spend a few bucks.

2. Successful managers spend about half of their time tending to current business and half of their time in search of new niches. Before this time allocation is possible, you must build a strong management team. Most owners believe they can't be away from the daily activities of their companies a few days each week. These "indispensable men" will likely never go niching. They will also fill the graveyard without creating substantial wealth.

3. Draw up lists of your company's core competencies and criteria for niches that will maximize them. This will enable you to know a promising niche when you see it or know what to do to make it one. Such a list will discipline you to focus on only the right opportunities.

4. Niching is not big-game hunting. It's listening to low-voiced comments and offhand questions from customers. Niche-aholics take what the market will give them, and in today's economy, that is either high volume but low profits or low volume but high profits. It's okay to hunt for niches with sales of $1 to $5 million. In some cases, it's the best strategy of all.

Midas Managers are not born, they are made. Some have to work at it awhile before they develop the Midas touch. It took Jack about 10 years of operating SMP to reinvent himself as a niche-aholic. But in so doing, he discovered the real truth about business owners: They make the most money when they stop doing and start thinking about what should be done.

INVESTMENT BANKER MAN

Translation: A revenue shortfall of 40% has caused a cash crunch; therefore, all buyers in and out of the industry will be contacted

15

The Day Brazil Called
A BUSINESS MODEL STRATEGY

Chester Mann sat behind his desk and wondered how the world had changed so much, so fast. He was majority owner of Mann Wood Products, a manufacturer of materials for homebuilders. When Chester took over the company from his father 10 years before, it was an integrated supplier that did everything from logging forests that it owned to sawing, chipping, kilning, planing and moulding all that wood. But then one day Brazil had called, and nothing had been the same since.

An Integrated Empire of Wood

Woody Mann founded Mann Wood Products in the late 1950s, at first just sawing high-grade logs into boards for use by the furniture industry. Everything that could be sawed could be sold, usually at a good margin. By the mid-1960s, Woody had added a couple of kilns so Mann could sell dry boards as well. The future looked bright, so he reinvested his considerable profits into the business, buying either equipment or acreage to help Mann Wood Products grow.

Soon, Woody had amassed a large portfolio of land, which was harvested by outside companies until Mann started its own logging operation. Next he added a chip mill, which ground small diameter branches and logs, also known as pulpwood, into small wood chips for use by big paper companies. And he added other value-added operations, such as planing (shaving boards to a finished product), moulding, and canting (parts for making pallets).

By the mid-1980s, Mann's process chain looked like this:

Mann Wood Products

Process Chain

The shaded boxes represent process steps that interfaced directly with customers; the unshaded boxes represent internal processes. Mann *owned* each process step in the most expensive sense of the word. There was a large fixed investment associated with every one: The sawmill cost about $4 million to build, the chip mill $6 million, and so on. In all, Woody had spent more than $25 million to build his empire.

By the time Chester took over the Company, Mann Wood Products was generating more than $85 million in annual sales and about $7 million in profits. Then he answered the fateful phone call.

Brazil on Line Two

It was a Friday morning. Chester was mentally preparing for his weekly golf game when his secretary said he had a call holding from an unknown sales rep. When Chester picked up, the voice on the other end indicated he was representing a Brazilian company's products in the U.S. It was part sales call, part courtesy call, since Mann already sold most of the products that the company was offering. But there was one major difference: price. If Chester was hearing correctly, Brazilian Forest Product's items were selling for about 15% less than Mann's manufacturing costs.

Chester immediately ordered small amounts of the range of products from the Brazilian company. After a fair amount of testing (and soul-searching), he decided that the wood from Brazil was at least as high-quality as Mann's. Brazilian Forest Products had stocked warehouses with wood across the U.S. This depot strategy assured adequate and timely delivery to customers.

The big question was what to do about the intruder. First came denial. Certainly Brazilian Forest Products couldn't sell at such low prices for the long-term, Chester reasoned. But a fair number of Mann's customers had noticed the low prices and switched to the less expensive wood and some had even signed long-term contracts. Second came anger. Why was this happening to him? Chester had done everything by the book, paid his dues, and mastered the forest products industry as well as anyone. He would show the Brazilians. He matched their prices board for board, even though it meant slashing his sales by one-third and turning Mann's black ink into red.

Third came acceptance. After a year of getting hammered by foreign competition, Mann was generating about $50 million in sales and $5 million in losses. Chester finally accepted that he must change strategies or risk losing his family business.

A New World

Chester studied Mann's process chain and made an adult decision: most of the steps had to go. He made a simple chart showing a reconceptualized chain.

Mann Wood Products
Reconceptualized Process Chain

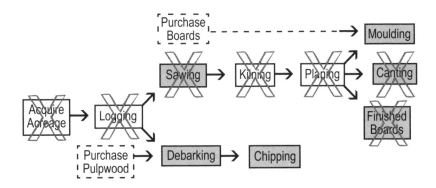

Chester would stop buying land, shut down the logging operation, the sawmill, the kilning, planing and canting operations. Mann would no longer manufacture boards; rather, it would buy them from Brazilian Forest Products, and the Brazilians new chief competitor, Argentinean Wood Products. Guessing that the Brazilians and Argentineans could not meet quick delivery schedules, Chester decided Mann would mould the boards for next day/next week delivery to home builders. He also started buying pulpwood from independent loggers to feed the chip mill. Mann's existing logging operation could not generate enough pulpwood on its own to justify its existence, but the large paper mills needed wood chips from regional sources, so they were willing to sign long-term supply contracts that were lucrative for Mann.

In the course of reconceptualizing his process chain, Chester had reduced Mann Wood Products to just two divisions: moulding and chipping.
This contraction was not without pain. The company wrote-off about $15
million in assets, reduced head count by more than 100, (including aunts,
uncles and cousins), and even forced Momma Mann to retire. Sales went
from $85 million at their zenith to just $22 million after the reorganization.
However, instead of losing $5 million per year, Mann was now earning $3.5
million.

After all of the dust had settled, so to speak, Chester was sanguine. He
was spending less time on the golf course and more time in the markets he
served. But he no longer waited for the phone to ring and change his life.
With his niche-based strategy, reconceptualized process chain. and long-term
supply agreements, he was the one making the calls.

BLUEPRINT

In most industries, globalization has blown up *supply chains*, which link sources and customers of products, services, finances, or information. Take the home building supply chain: trees are grown; logs are harvested and processed; wood is delivered to builders who construct the house. Each party to the supply chain has its own process chain that holds the activities it undertakes to serve its customers.

In an always-on global economy, managing your supply chain and process chain has become a vital endeavor. Competition is giving way to collaboration. This was evident in the story of Mann Wood Products, which might be referred to as "forced" collaboration. Once global suppliers enter a market, U.S. firms must decide whether to compete or collaborate. Mann Wood Products tried competing before deciding it was in its best interest to use the Brazilian products. For most owners, the notion that working with your competition will actually help create wealth for both parties is counterintuitive, but it can be nonetheless true.

Managing a supply chain is not easy. "Unforced" collaboration occurs when companies work together for mutual benefit. This enables supply chain partners to leverage each other's operational capabilities so that in combination they perform better than they could individually. *Co-opetition* can occur anywhere along the supply chain, from design to deliver, which lets everyone maximize their capabilities. But collaboration means sharing information and ideas, which is not exactly easy for business owners.

Managing a process chain is also challenging. As discussed in Chapter 13, process steps that rely on intellectual capital should be owned while other steps can be merely controlled via outsourcing. Outsourcing may or may not involve offshoring, a fancy word for using suppliers from foreign countries where labor may be cheaper. Most small-to-mid-sized private company owners shy away from offshoring, since it takes skills and resources they don't possess.

Even outsourcing within the U.S., inshoring if you will, can be a challenge. First, you have to foster relationships with prospective outsourcers. Second, you have to establish expectations and quality control programs that protect everyone's interests. Third, you have to keep communication channels open so both parties can leverage each other's capabilities. All of this requires developing and perfecting new skill sets. For instance, think how hard it is to assure 100 percent quality within facilities that you own, then multiply that by three.

Imagine a world where almost all companies have rationalized their process chains and most supply chains are adding value because the players are maximizing their activities. This is occurring right now, and it's bad news for companies whose work is dominated by non-value adding process steps. Such underperforming companies will not be invited into important supply chains, leaving more opportunities for value-adding players. Most automotive suppliers, for example, would rather supply Toyota and Honda than General Motors and Ford. That's because the former's supply chains are profitable while the latter's are not, and value-adding participants in a profitable supply chain are "allowed" to make money.

The following steps can be used to rationalize your supply and process chains:

1. Gain entry into profitable supply chains. Start by offering innovative and value-adding services to the supply chain you want to penetrate. This is an area where strategic thinking is important. It might take years of planning.

2. Be prepared to answer these questions: 1) Are you willing to share strategic information, responsibilities, and resources with your supply chain partners; and 2) Are you willing to integrate operationally with other firms, even competitors, to enhance the performance and responsiveness of the supply chain? The answer to both better be "yes."

3. Review each process step and determine if it has a positive value proposition. Own steps that rely on intellectual capital and outsource, if possible, the rest. (See Chapter 13).

4. Design modular processes with maximum interchangeability. Simplified processes are both effective and easy to outsource, so they work for most everyone. One caveat: it may be necessary to hire a "manager of design and outsourcing."

5. Once you've recognized that your supply chain has changed for good, make the tough decision to exit process steps at which you aren't adding value. Chester basically withdrew from all process steps involved with producing boards, parts of the business that his father had spent years building. This takes tremendous courage.

The globalization of our economy has changed the rules of business. Optimizing your company's process and supply chains is critical to success. In fact, there are few more crucial roles for a manager today.

16

Productize or Die!

A BUSINESS MODEL STRATEGY

Most investment bankers want to own and operate their own business. They're used to assisting companies late in the owner's career when the business is humming and there's no sign of the 20 years or so of hard work that it took to get it that way. After a career advising such owners, banker Don Knight was no exception. While Don respected his clients, he did not think they were more talented than he. So when he had a chance, he made the leap into business ownership.

From a fraternity brother, Don learned that a Fortune 500 company had decided to divest a number of non-core divisions, including one located in his town. The division, Automated Inc., distributed vision and motion controls used to automate industrial activities. For several years, it had been breaking even on about $10 million in annual revenue. While it had no proprietary products, it had some geographic protection for several of its product lines. But when the parent had tried to sell Automated via a standard Wall Street auction, there were no takers.

Don decided to make a play for it. He offered book value for Automated. After three months of negotiations, the parent company agreed to sell the division for $4 million, or about 15 percent above book value, and Don became a business owner. He financed the deal using a $2 million asset-based loan and a $2 million seller note and invested $400,000 of his own money to support working capital. Little did he know that $400,000 would be barely enough to keep the company going longer than six months.

Life as an Owner

Don should have known that no matter how much he studied a company or its industry, he wouldn't actually be able to grasp the opportunity until he owned it. Unfortunately, then it would be too late, since he would be stuck with the investment. This is what happened with Automated. During the year before the sale, the parent company had cut off support for the division and several key employees had quit. The market had softened and globalization was pushing the industry overseas and putting the hurt on domestic suppliers.

During the first four months that Don owned it, Automated lost $50,000 per month. That cut its cash on hand by two-thirds to just $100,000 (it had cost $100,000 to close the transaction, leaving starting working capital of $300,000). Don was feeling the heat. So he did what all first-time owners do: cut his staff.

Releasing eight out of 50 employees lessened the monthly losses but didn't solve the ultimate problem. The margins on a number of products were declining. Items such as programmable logic controllers were becoming commodities, and many of Automated's other products could be ordered off the Internet for much less from competitors. Yet Automated didn't even have a Web site.

And in a period of soft sales, Automated hemorrhaged cash. There were eight outside salespeople (supported by five sales coordinators) and four inside salespeople. There were five engineers with substantial product knowledge, and a sizeable clerical staff. Everyone was on salary and the salespeople also got bonuses based on the total gross margin dollars earned on the products they sold.

To survive and eventually create value, Don needed to move Automated away from its "wait until the customer calls" marketing model. As a project engineering company, it was similar to a machine shop or a contractor. That is, it had no recurring revenue stream. Don needed to reconceptualize the entire business model.

Intellectual Capital Inventory

Step one was to take stock of the intellectual capital, or know-how, that existed inside Automated. Leveraging that resource would be the basis for reconceptualizing the model. Of course, Don had never worked in the controls industry, so he didn't know exactly what Automated had. But after dozens of conversations with engineers and salespeople, he determined that the company housed substantial know-how. Automated's core competencies included the ability to integrate components into a turnkey solution, especially when wireless transmission and remote control were involved. Automated had completed a number of interesting engineering projects through the years, which included:

- A bar code tunnel for managing inventory in a plant
- A controller for managing activities in a greenhouse, including lighting and watering
- A system that uses wireless networks to control nearly every machine in a factory

After hearing about numerous successful engineering projects, a thought occurred to Don: Why not package some of them into brands? Then Automated could sell the wheel, instead of constantly reinventing it.

Don quickly developed a process for productizing Automated's engineering projects. Recognizing that the key to reconceptualizing the business model was to organize people around a new goal, he created a SWAT team and gave it the following tasks:

Automated Inc.

SWAT Team Functions

1. Identify a project to productize and brand
2. Perform an analysis to determine market size, pricing, and path to customers
3. Analyze the cost structure of the branded product
4. Conceptualize the process chain (how it will be made, marketed and sold)
5. Create a pro forma income statement for it.

Don wanted to manage this process, so he designated himself the SWAT team leader. To show the importance of this role to the future of the company, he adopted the title "Manager of New Ideas." Speed to market was vital, so Don gave the team just three months to work through the five steps the first time. After that, it would be as easy as repeating those steps again and again. Don called this the "Head & Shoulders Approach:" Rinse, Lather, Repeat.

Needing a Hit

Don had stanched Automated's bleeding, but he felt a sense of urgency about the launch of its first branded product. He needed a hit. The team had chosen a waste water treatment controller, which allowed almost lights-out remote control of chemicals and flow at small, non-municipal waste water treatment facilities. Automated had created this product a couple of years before for a private company that owned a handful of these plants.

This was just the sort of niche market that appealed to Don. It was practically hiding in plain sight. After studying the private waste water treatment market, he believed that at least 5,000 such facilities existed in the U.S. About a dozen private companies owned large numbers of these plants, giving Automated a ready-made group of major customers to target.

Branding was key because it would enable Automated to market and sell packaged solutions rather than one-off projects. Branding would also differentiate Automated's offerings and help them earn a big return on its investment. Don named the first product "Sentry," which connoted a system that worked 24/7 without supervision.

Most of the potential customers for Sentry were managing their facilities with on-site staff using analog computer systems. Don figured Sentry would save them each at least $50,000 per year in labor (the approximate cost of one on-site technician). Aiming to give buyers a six- to nine-month payback, he settled on a price of $30,000 per installation.

Could Automated make money at this price? The answer was "yes," mainly because the engineering was already paid for and most of the process chain outsourced. Outsourcing saved cash (which was still in short supply) and enabled Sentry's sales to scale.

The following shows the new product's process chain:

Sentry Process Chain

Market → Sell → Produce → Integrate → Install → Maintain

Automated would own the white process steps and outsource the shaded ones. Figuring that marketing and selling Sentry were proprietary steps and therefore should be owned, Don hired two dedicated marketers and three salespeople. He outsourced each of the remaining steps — producing the individual products, integrating the result, and installing and maintaining the systems — to multiple vendors.

The average total cost for the three steps was $15,000 per unit plus any necessary maintenance in the first six months after installation. Don created the following income statement, based on Automated selling 100 Sentry systems the first year:

Sentry Pro Forma Income Statement

Revenues (100 units * $30,000)	$3,000,000
Cost of Sales (100 units * $15,000)	1,500,000
Gross Profit	$1,500,000
SG&A	500,000
Pre-tax Profit	$1,000,000

By just selling 100 units per year, Automated could earn $1 million. After Year 1, Don believed it could sell at least 200 per year.

A Whole New Company

As it turned out, Automated sold that many in the first 12 months. The company earned almost $2 million that year with just six employees dedicated to Sentry.

Based on that success, Don quickly converted Automated into a branded control systems marketing company. The SWAT team did its job, even though some of the projects it chose to productize never made it to market. By using a replicable process, it could decide quickly whether or not to move forward. And by outsourcing steps in its process chain where it couldn't add value, the company could scale up quickly, Within three years, Automated was marketing four branded control systems. Each had potential annual sales of $5 million to $10 million and pre-tax profit margins of 20 to 25 percent.

In a few short though sometimes painful years, Don had totally reconceptualized Automated's business model. Instead of selling project engineering by the hour, it was now selling branded products by the truckload. Thus Don's mantra: "Impact over hours!" Don continued to employ engineers to handle custom jobs, but these projects were really just feedstock for Automated's next branded products.

By the third year of ownership, Don possessed a whole new respect for his fellow business managers. He finally understood why most owners look totally exhausted much of the time. But he also felt a jolt of pride. Because, unlike the majority of managers, Don chose to productize, rather than die.

BLUEPRINT

Most companies do not have recurring revenue and income streams. Because of this, whether they're contractors, distributors, or retailers, they have difficulty creating value. This was the challenge at Automated Inc. until Don Knight began productizing.

Productizing is difficult yet it's sometimes absolutely necessary. It requires a strategic approach to the business; the owner has to work on the company – not in it. The goal is to get the business to work productively *without the owner*, which most owners would find challenging and scary. Yet enough owners convert their companies into "franchise" type operations to make it a real possibility for everyone.

This is not to say that every company should be a franchisor. Rather, the goal of every owner should be to institutionalize the business to the point where its model can be easily replicated. This requires the creation of a system that works as seamlessly as Don's "Head & Shoulders." But even service businesses can productize and brand their offerings (think H&R Block).

Branding was critical to Automated's success. There are a number of ways to define branding, but my favorite goes like this: developing a name that identifies the product or service, differentiates it from the competition, and creates value for the customer and the company. Branding achieved several goals that helped Don to convert a money-losing business into a wealth-creating entity:

- It allowed Automated to market packaged, turnkey solutions that solved customers' problems, i.e., sell the wheel and not the designs to the wheel.
- It set Automated's offerings apart from what its competitors were selling.

- It conveyed value with a proposition that Automated's products paid for themselves in less than two years.
- It gave the company a focal point, which made the company's strategic shift easier for project-oriented engineers to get behind.

Don also came up with a company slogan that captured its new focus on branded control products.

The following steps can be used to implement the "productization" strategy:

1. Take inventory of your company's skill sets, core competencies, and intellectual capital. Selling the wheel begins with leveraging this know-how.

2. Form a team to identify and analyze opportunities to productize.

3. Test the return on investment for each new product to make sure it meets your minimum return needs (see Chapter 20 for a complete discussion on how to measure returns).

4. Re-launch as a niche-based company that focuses on products based on its core competencies.

5. Develop a franchising mindset. Imagine replicating your strategy 100 times over. Can it be done? In other words, do you have systems in place to create and manage 100 branded products?

As Don Knight found out, a business owner's ultimate responsibility is to create a condition where the day-to-day success of the company doesn't depend on him or her. Only the owner can position the business to sell the wheel again and again.

17

Push or Pull?

A BUSINESS MODEL STRATEGY

Business owner J.T. Sanders felt like he was living a Dickens novel: it had been the best of times for him and his company; it had been the worst of times.

DynaBuild Inc. (DBI) designed and manufactured steel buildings using a proprietary metal stud technology. The worst of times had been the first 10 years in business. J.T. thought he was doing everything right, but the dawning of the Conceptual Age had turned his business and his industry upside-down. He hadn't been prepared for changing times. But the best of times weren't far off. In just 24 months, J.T. was able to reconceptualize his business model, ensuring that DBI could thrive for years to come.

The Push

J.T. began his engineering career with a company that manufactured specialty metals. Through a series of jobs, he learned how to bend and cut just about any type of metal. Along the way, he managed a project making metal studs for use in high-end homes. J.T.'s entire life changed as a result of that project. Having built homes on the side, he immediately saw the benefits of an integrated framing system designed around light-gauge steel members. Within a year he quit his engineering job and founded DBI.

J.T. quickly designed three metal-frame homes and offered them to the market. His homes had several advantages over traditional stick-built houses. They were uniformly constructed and not subject to variances often found in wood studs. They would not rot or succumb to termites. And once a homebuilder knew how to work with steel, it was actually 10 to 20 percent cheaper to construct an edifice than wood.

This last advantage determined DBI's path to market. Since DBI could not afford to design, manufacture, and build homes, it had to rely on independent homebuilders to handle the last step. They would be DBI's dealers. The company shipped its homes as complete kits that the builder assembled, almost by numbers: Metal member "1" was riveted to member "2," and so on.

Although this sounded simple enough, it was a different approach than what most builders were used to and thus created a learning curve. They often had to get four or five homes under their belts before they reaped the full cost savings of DBI's system. J.T. needed to find and train dealers who would stick with steel long enough to realize its benefits. Further, he would have to support them with extensive technical and marketing assistance. DBI would only be as successful as its dealers let it become.

J.T. spent 75 percent of his time building out DBI's dealer network. After 10 years he had signed up 50 homebuilders, mainly in Southern states, where steel's advantages were more accepted by the marketplace than in other regions. Each dealer sold an average of eight homes per year, which generated average sales to DBI of $30,000 per home. A decade in, the company was bringing in $12 million in annual revenue and about $1 million in profits.

Then it happened. The double whammy of 9/11, which stalled the economy, and globalization, which jacked up steel prices. Homebuilding in the U.S. slowed, but China was still sucking up enough steel from U.S. producers to raise the cost of the remaining domestic supply by 30 percent. All of a sudden DBI's steel framing packages were more expensive than competing materials by 10 to 20 percent. Most of its dealers gravitated back to wood.

The Pull

Within two years, DBI's sales fell 50 percent, causing the company's first million-dollar loss. Something had to change or it would soon be out of business. J.T. had to change the physics of his business.

He started by scrapping DBI's business model. Now, instead of *pushing* his products onto the market, he would let them be *pulled*. But this required re-thinking the company's entire marketing model.

J.T. had learned several things about marketing his buildings over the prior 10 years. First, relying on independent dealers for DBI's sales was a risk he couldn't afford to take any longer. They had motives that were more important to them than DBI's success, and rightfully so. Second, most home buyers were not wedded to steel framing. They usually chose the least expensive house that met their needs.

But there were a few buyers who wanted steel, even if it cost more. J.T. wanted those synergistic buyers pulling DBI's products to market. The first pull market was actually uncovered by one of his dealers. She had figured out that steel framing was especially well-suited for small churches and had located and trained a group of volunteers that erected them for needy congregations. With free labor, DBI's buildings were competitive regardless of the cost of steel. So J.T. created a joint venture with her to brand and build a church business for DBI. Within a year, it was shipping 15 churches per month and earning margins that on their own made the company profitable.

J.T.'s second attempt involved marketing through the Internet. Thinking that if prospects could price customized homes on DBI's Web site, it would open up a major market, he hired a software developer in Costa Rica. The developer built a platform program that loaded most of DBI's engineering and costs onto its Web site. Although that gave competitors a view into DBI's capabilities, J.T. felt it was a small price to pay, and he was right.

Soon, the Web site had attracted a community of users who interacted with the platform and helped improve it and improve DBI's products. For instance, the site was changed when user's asked for an interface to a 3-D modeling software program. All of this was a revelation for J.T.: information about products was no longer owned and distributed by companies; with the Internet, it was now in the hands of millions of individuals.

J.T. called the Web site his magic show. The cost of maintaining it was minimal and yet it generated substantial profits. More importantly, it pulled DBI into the entire market. By the second year, DBI was filling 10 online orders a month.

The third pull market appeared via a group of 50 architects in Florida who had years of experience putting high-end steel-framed houses in the ground. It turned out that wealthy home buyers liked the safety and security of steel bones, and these architects had cracked the code on how to market to them. J.T. offered to enhance his Internet software to enable the architects to manage projects and commit DBI to a cost structure. In return, DBI got to be their exclusive steel framing supplier. The architects agreed, and soon they were placing orders for four or five large homes per month at revenues to DBI approaching $100,000 apiece.

Exploiting this last market required J.T. to change his thinking about business. He had always been told that the best way to deal with uncertainty was to increase control over all of your resources. In fact, all of J.T.'s role models were unabashed control freaks. The architects pulled J.T. in a different direction. Now he had to relinquish control and instead rely on their initiative to identify and assemble resources for him. In other words, instead of dictating solutions, he needed to listen to his community of users and react accordingly. He had to let himself be pulled into the market.

By the end of the second year, J.T.'s new mindset had helped DBI reach $20 million in annual sales and $4 million in profits. Pushing its products onto the market had forced the company to rely on dealers who ultimately had conflicts of interest. The pull approach leveraged the motives of players whose interests were in alignment with DBI's because they needed its products. It took a few years, but J.T. Sanders reconceptualized his view of business, which led to a reconceptualization of his company's business model, which ultimately pulled him to financial independence.

BLUEPRINT

A wise business owner once told me that successful service providers create a condition where the door to their office swings in, not the other way around. In other words, the clients come to them. A pull business model creates this condition.

Pull business models first appeared in the 1950s with *just-in-time* manufacturing processes that ordered inventory as it was needed. That caused a big improvement in efficiency over push models that called for ordering certain lot sizes regardless of demand. More recently, *lean* processes have created even greater efficiency in supply and process chains, thanks to communications tools like the Internet that enable companies to collaborate like never before.

The Internet provides the backbone for communities to coalesce around ideas. Look no further than the development of Linux, the open-source computer operating system, to see how thousands of users can work together for a common good. Knowledge creation now transcends company boundaries. In fact, innovation and creativity are being distributed across firms with the idea that if two heads are better than one, then a million heads should be the goal. But achieving this requires platforms that harness common interests.

Pull models are increasingly vital due to the uncertainty caused by globalization. The Conceptual Age rewards companies that empower their communities to pull what they want rather than push their way into the market with a command-and-control mindset.

The following table shows a comparison between push and pull business models:

Push Models	Pull Models
Centralized control	Decentralized control
Restricted participation	Open participation
Assume demand is predictable	Assume demand is uncertain
Resource-centric	People-centric
Efficiency focus	Innovation focus

The idea that to get more out of a business model you need to give up control is highly counter-intuitive. But by sharing tools that once were considered proprietary, a multitude of players can advance a common cause. J.T. shared DBI's engineering software openly with the market in hopes that a diverse group of buyers would not only emerge but also help make the platform more effective. That is exactly what happened.

The nature of strategy changes in a pull environment. Instead of depending on resources owned within your company, it requires the ability to identify, mobilize, and integrate others' resources to add value for your customers. Each company needs to maximize its intellectual capital and tap others to do what it can't (another way of describing the design and deliver model in Chapter 13). In the Conceptual Age, winners play to their strengths but are quick to leverage others' strengths, too.

The following steps can be used to create a pull business model:

1. Determine how to make your door swing inward. Who needs your products or services to meet their goals?

2. Create a platform that organizes and feeds a niched, networked community of these potential customers. Give them enough value-adding tools
   – without restrictions – to collaborate and innovate. Make them believe
   it's in their best interests to contribute something of value to the community.

3. Collaborate with partners. Leverage your partners' unique intellectual
   capital to build your platform. Choosing, enticing, and rewarding partners is a key to success in the Conceptual Age.

4. Dare to share. Innovation within networks occurs when the companies
   with platforms share capabilities. This is difficult for many business
   owners because they were taught to shield anything proprietary from
   outsiders. But in the Conceptual Age, competition is not the central constraint; it's the manager's ability to conceptualize value-added solutions.

Robert F. Kennedy popularized the curse: "May you live in interesting
times." The Conceptual Age certainly qualifies. The job of every owner and
manager is to make them productive times as well.

18

The Instant Company

A BUSINESS MODEL STRATEGY

More crazy notions seem to originate in California than any other place on earth. One July 4th, L.A.'s Karen Swanson had one of her own. Karen, an unemployed marketing executive, announced to no one in particular that she was going to launch a line of fashion sandals and have them in stores for spring.

Her husband immediately tried to throw cold water on her plans. Karen had no designs for the sandals, no factory to manufacture them, no path to the mass market, and no company to make all of this happen, he argued. And then there was the timing. To debut next spring, Karen would have to take orders from retail chains by New Year's Day, which was less than five months away. As the prosecutor rested his case, Karen surprised him by admitting that everything he had just said was true. But, she added, none of it was going to slow her down.

Building an Instant Company

Karen was not without weapons. Her 15 years in marketing with Nike had taught her many things. First, and most importantly, she knew there was a market for dress sandals from two studies she had overseen, though Nike's top brass had never wanted want to pursue it. Second, Karen had contacts in the shoe industry around the world and believed she could marshal the necessary resources to launch her company, which she dubbed HipFlops. Finally, Karen was at that age when you either pursued your own course or signed up for corporate life for good. When she left Nike three months before, she vowed never to return to a big company, and she had the energy and drive to keep that promise. Fortunately, Nike stock had done well of late and she also had a few hundred thousand dollars in the bank.

Karen's first step toward realizing her American dream was lining up a designer for the line of sandals. While at Nike, she had worked with more than a dozen design houses and thus knew who could help. She chose a small shop in Seattle – Too Cool Designs — that could move from idea-to-blueprint at warp speed, and, more importantly, had strong relationships with several manufacturers in China.

Karen supplied Too Cool with a few sketches and the designers snapped into action. Within three days they had created eight different looks. To share ideas, work and supporting data, they used Basecamp, a Web-based program that linked everyone involved in the project. Karen reviewed the designs and selected several to have made into prototypes. They, along with specifications and materials, were uploaded to Basecamp so that once Karen chose a manufacturing partner in China, that company could access them, too.

Outsourcing to China

Outsourcing a product to China can be a daunting task. The language, culture, and regulations couldn't be more different from what Americans are accustomed to. Karen knew from experience that manufacturing sandals in the U.S. would cost about $7 per pair versus about $2 per pair to make them in China and ship them to L.A. China was the obvious choice.

Too Cool introduced Karen to two manufacturers in China. Karen had been to China numerous times while working for Nike, so she already had relationships with several firms there as well. With prototypes in hand and the designs already sent digitally to the candidates, Karen headed east.

Unlike most Americans who travel to China for business, Karen knew what to expect. She understood that *guanxi* (pronounced gwan shee), a deeply-held relationship built in a slow purposeful way, was extremely important there. In a country without a strong commercial legal system, guanxi fills the void. Chinese businesspeople honor relationships; that is, as long as the relationship is more valuable than the transaction.

Negotiating with the Chinese is also an unusual experience. Chinese businesspeople will often attempt to control the meeting place and schedule, sometimes use friendships to extract concessions, and aren't above displays of anger. Believing that Westerners are constantly in a hurry, they will try to wear their visitors down as if waging a war of attrition. It is typical, almost expected, for the Chinese to renegotiate a deal on the final day of the process. Once negotiations are complete, they might sign a contract only to humor their guests. To the Chinese, a completed contract often serves as a beginning point for future negotiations.

Karen had a strategy to deal with all of this. She supplied a prototype with clear and specific conditions of doing business with her to each of the five prospective manufacturers. The provisions included material and size specifications for the sandals as well as payment requirements. This last point was particularly important to Karen. She needed 90 days to convert the sandals into cash. Fortunately, most business in China is done using long payment terms, so this was not a stumbling block, but she still needed to arrange letters of credit for the goods from an international bank.

Karen then ran an auction to help her choose among the suppliers. Each was led to believe that another manufacturer was winning. She told them that she needed to hear their best deal or they risked losing the opportunity. The maneuvering went on for a couple of weeks until Karen chose Kong Manufacturing in Shanghai.

Aside from offering her great pricing and competitive terms, Kong employed several sales reps whose English and knowledge of U.S. protocols were almost equal to her own. Kong assigned Julie Chen to the HipFlops account. Julie coordinated all activities and communications between the two companies. Other than the shipping time, buying from Kong was no different than dealing with vendors in Los Angeles. Sixty days later, finished sandals in a multitude of sizes danced off the production lines in China, and the calendar hadn't flipped to September yet.

The Hype Thing

Of course, making sandals was only half the battle: Karen also had to sell them. She didn't have the money to build a brand in the traditional way, and besides, traditional brand-building techniques weren't going to support the hyper-growth she expected. She needed to create hype, so she hired a firm that specialized in viral marketing via hipster websites and blogs, including ones that catered to Californians' obsession with sandals.

Within weeks more than 100 sites were praising HipFlops and generating demand. The hype drove substantial business to HipFlops' Web site, and by January, the company was averaging more than $100,000 per month in sales. But Karen also wanted to peddle her sandals through some niche retail chains. To accomplish this she used more traditional brand-building techniques, including leveraging old relationships, granting exclusive territories in select areas, and selling enforced scarcity. It didn't hurt that people were walking into shoe stores and asking for HipFlops.

In its first year, Karen's instant company pulled in $14 million in sales. In Year 2, it almost doubled that, despite employing just eight people. HipFlops outsourced design, manufacturing, most marketing, and delivery of its products, all of which its employees coordinated smoothly with some savvy use of technology. In fact, that's practically all they did. As Karen celebrated the second anniversary of her crazy notion, she was struck by how much she had accomplished in such a short period of time — with a little help from the "world is flat" global economy. Best of all, her doubting husband was finally speechless.

BLUEPRINT

In the Conceptual Age, small and mid-sized companies have a major advantage over their larger competitors. At a time when supply and demand are constantly and rapidly changing, smaller companies are not burdened by high fixed overhead nor fixed ways of thinking. And thanks to outsourcing, resources not previously available to small companies are now accessible to those with the imagination to use them. Those two factors, combined with the speed of communications and collaboration on the Internet, have made instant companies possible.

Every instant company starts with an idea for a hit product or service. Most wannabe entrepreneurs stop there because moving forward is fraught with difficulty and uncertainty. In effect, these people create their own walls. However, a few adventurers jump over the wall and some are very successful. But anyone can do it, which I learned from Frank Helms. Frank is the CEO of Helms Printing, a $30 million-a-year family business that specializes in sophisticated printing techniques. Several years ago, Frank handed off daily management and now spends his days acting as a "mini-JP Morgan," as he calls it, launching instant companies based on technologies and services that are strategic for his company. For instance, an inventor who had patented a new sublimation process recently approached him. Rather than acquire it and let the project get bogged down within Helms Printing, Frank organized a new company to take advantage of the opportunity. He then allocated the necessary resources, forged the necessary relationships, and oversaw the implementation of systems that enabled it to flourish. Poof! Instant company.

As soon as one such company is established and successful, he goes to the next one. Once he gets a company to $5 to $10 million in revenues, he sells it and adds to his nest egg. But in almost every case, Helms Printing also benefits, whether through a technology exchange, the opening of a new market niche, or the opportunity to supply printing services to the instant company.

More and more small business owners are attempting to do business around the world, especially in China. There are lots of little things to learn: Having your business card printed with the local dialect on one side and English on the other, presenting your card with both hands, reading your host's card before placing it in front of you, and so on. You have to consider how to handle the big differences, too, like being a patient negotiator, playing competitors off each other, and being willing to cut your losses and go home empty-handed. The idea of building deep relationships before doing business, or what the Chinese call guanxi, may seem downright 19th Century to Americans, but it's absolutely necessary for success over in the Middle Kingdom.

The following steps can be used to create an instant company:

1. Come up with a big idea. I would wager that each year, every adult in America generates one or two ideas with the potential to be big hits in the market. Most of these ideas are spawned from the inability to find the solution to a particular problem. This is the point where most people fall victim to the "only one" syndrome; that is, they believe they must be the only ones in the world who need that product or service. But with seven billion people roaming the planet, there's a pretty good chance that at least a niche market exists.

2. Design at warp speed. If you don't get to market quickly, competitors will likely spot the same market deficiency or consumer tastes will change and eliminate it altogether. Instant companies require instant design. If a product is involved, sketch the vision and then get help from an expert creating a design and commissioning a prototype. If it's a service, choose a firm that specializes in process design.

3. Organize on the Internet. One of the keys to success with an instant company is to make the process steps systematic. Life-cycle management applications like Basecamp let you leverage existing intellectual capital rather than re-inventing the wheel. Plus, since most are Web-based, they have a built-in backbone for worldwide, instantaneous communication and collaboration.

4. Move quickly into production. Producing your product or service has to happen fast, too. Find the right factory through referrals or research, but make sure it can coordinate activities amongst you and your partners. No matter how experienced it is, expect to engage in trial and error. Mr. Murphy (of what can go wrong, will go wrong fame) will likely show up early and often. The key is to react quickly with an almost insane sense of urgency.

5. Feed the hype machine. Real-time, all-the-time hype is the order of the day. America's attention deficit disorder is amazing. The instant company strategy exploits this malady, but don't try it on your own. Techniques like viral marketing have become sophisticated disciplines and you should outsource this step to those who specialize in it.

6. Take what the market will give you. Nearly all instant companies are born to take advantage of an unmet need. Once you've filled this niche, look for another one. What goes up quickly may come down just as fast. Security is knowing you can launch instant companies in a systematic way again and again.

Karen Swanson acted on a seemingly ridiculous notion. It probably couldn't have been helped, since she was from California and all. Most people in her life thought she was crazy because they would never attempt such a thing. But she knew that a thin line separates a great idea from a total waste of time. The major difference is the amount of sales each generates.

Midas Managers are contrarians by nature. They intuitively understand that if you go with the pack, you'll get pack returns,. For Karen, the new queen of the sandal business, those just weren't good enough.

Part IV

PRIVATE FINANCE

19

Raise Your Private Finance IQ

Private finance, which explains the investment and financial behavior of players in private capital markets, is a new field of study. Up until now, private companies have been viewed as the unruly stepchildren of public markets. Occasionally, a select few come of age and are allowed to eat at the grownup table, but the rest aren't considered mature enough to converse with.

Studying private companies is long overdue. They comprise over 99 percent of the businesses on earth yet receive barely a notice from academics. Most academics pay attention to only those private companies that will soon go public. This book, like *Private Capital Markets* before it, demonstrates that private markets are standalone entities with a unique body of knowledge that explains their structure and operation. Creating wealth in unique markets requires unique strategies. But a central premise of this book is that just knowing private finance can lead to wealth creation.

Because of their lack of finance education and training, most business owners tip over the three-legged stool of business. Typically, they'll have a handle on the first two legs (marketing and operations) thanks to what they've learned in the school of hard knocks. The third leg (finance) is usually left to the company's controller or outsourced to a CPA. In either event, it's not finance that's practiced, but accounting. What's the difference? Accounting deals with costs; finance deals with values. Business owners need to respect each discipline, but creating value is fundamentally a finance activity.

Private finance rests on three pillars:

- Value relativity. Private business value is based on the reason for the appraisal. The reason gives rise to a value world where a unique value for that business is calculated. Thus, there are as many correct values for a business at any one point in time as there are reasons for an appraisal.

- Cost of capital and value-creation. Business value is not created until a company generates returns on invested capital in excess of its cost of capital. Therefore, owners need to maximize their company's returns while minimizing its cost of capital.

- Business owners choose their company's transfer value. Business transfer comprises a spectrum of alternatives, not just a traditional sale. In fact, there are hundreds of transfer methods. Here's the key insight: The choice of transfer method determines the value world. So once an owner chooses a transfer method, she has also chosen the value at which her business will be transferred.

Knowing these pillars opens up a whole new world of financial decision-making. Simply better understanding valuation can create wealth for an owner, for instance. Value worlds are conceptual realms where business value is measured and created. Think of them as planets in the universe. Each has a unique atmosphere, gravity, land mass, and so on, and survival on each requires an understanding of all of these unique physical properties.

Value worlds are similar in that each is governed by appraisal rules that are specific to that world and will generate a unique value. For instance, if you landed on the world of market value, you would be subject to the rules of the open market. This is the world in which most business owners would like to create value. But success in this world, as in all others, is predicated on understanding the rules and playing by them well.

It is possible to create wealth by planning or buying in one value world and then selling in another. For example, buying a business in the bankruptcy world and selling in the market value world usually creates wealth. Planning in the fair market value world and then going public in the IPO world also creates wealth.

This section contains five story chapters:

Chapter 20: To Buy or Not to Buy

A fundamental decision every manager faces is whether to commit financial resources to a person, place or thing. Should I hire that person? Should I purchase a building or rent? Should I buy that piece of equipment? This chapter provides a way to calculate whether an investment decision will add value to the business.

Chapter 21: The Value of Investment

The owner featured in this chapter demonstrates how to use Private Finance IQ to achieve returns in excess of his company's cost of capital. By requiring a return on the investment in his employees and tying their billing directly to how much wealth they are creating, this owner has created an effective, transparent, and very valuable business model.

Chapter 22: An Owner's Perspective On Value

You can walk into any private business in America and within 30 seconds correctly determine the market value of the firm. How? Just ask the owner and then divide by two (actually multiply by .7 and you typically have the right answer). But it is possible to transfer a business in the richer world of owner value, and this chapter shows how it's done.

Chapter 23: Sharing the Wealth

Many business owners want to transfer part of their wealth to future generations of their families. This chapter shows an effective way to accomplish that goal by planning in the world of fair market value and selling in the world of market value.

Chapter 24: Go Public Young Man

Going public isn't for everyone. Between the costs of complying with the Sarbanes-Oxley law and the hassle of answering to a multitude of shareholders, running a public company can be an enormous challenge. However, in the right situations, it can also be extremely lucrative. This chapter describes the human side of the initial public offering process.

Chapter 25: The Nucor Way

Although not officially part of this section, Chapter 25, The Nucor Way, is summarized here. In so many ways, Nucor Steel is an outlier of a company. In the real world, it has positively differentiated itself from all other steel companies. It is the lone public company profiled in this book. Once you read *The Nucor Way*, you'll know why it deserves to be described in these pages.

Nucor Steel is a Midas company, created by a Midas Manager of the first degree, Ken Iverson. He designed Nucor in his image — unassuming, egoless, and extremely productive — with a business model that aligns shareholder, management, and employee interests better than at any other company in the world. This strategy is available to all managers, if you have the guts to check your ego at the door.

This section of the book will help you raise your Private Finance IQ. In the global economy, managers must arm themselves with better financial weapons than in the past. Gut feel and payback still have a place in the thought process, but knowledge of value worlds, cost of capital, and transfer methods will lead to better decision-making, and ultimately, greater wealth.

INVESTMENT BANKER MAN

Commercial truth-in-lending — when prime hits 30%

20

To Buy or Not to Buy

A PRIVATE FINANCE STRATEGY

Sometimes the simplest problems are the hardest to solve. At least, that's what Jennifer Moehringer was beginning to think.

Jen had left a national staffing company 10 years before to start Permanent Staffing, and founding her own business had turned out to be a good decision. She had built Permanent into a solid niche player with annual revenues approaching $6 million. But the same problem she faced when she made the decision to go into business was once again troubling her: How do you know if the choices you're making are financially sound? How do you know if they are going to add value, and if so, how much? Jen knew she made decisions every day without any idea of whether they made financial sense for her business. There must be a better way, she thought.

So Jen asked a few other business owners how they made important investment choices. All gave the same answer — payback. The payback method was a tried-and-true friend of small business owners. It tells you simply how long it will take to get your money back from an investment. For example, if a project is going to cost $300,000 and it will add $100,000 in income per year, the payback will take three years.

Easy enough, thought Jen. But she had a nagging feeling that this method did not tell the whole story. For instance, there was no accounting for project risk or the time value of money. There had to be a better way, she thought again.

Fortunately, Jen was a lifelong student. She figured that a straightforward question such as how to determine whether a new salesperson will create value would be addressed in the first chapter of most finance textbooks. One afternoon in the local library dashed these hopes. Were all finance books written by professors who had never owned a small business? They were full of concepts that managers of large public companies might use, such as whether a market was efficient or how to determine yields on public securities; but nothing for her. Never one to give up, Jen finally found something near the middle of one book that might have been useful in her situation, if only she could figure it out.

Present Value

Jen had stumbled onto the concept of "present value." Present value describes how much something you receive in the future is worth in today's dollars. To calculate present value, Jen had to discount, or "reverse compound," the expected future value of her investment. This requires a discount rate, which is the same as the percentage return Jen needed to make on an investment given the risk.

Jen put pencil to paper. She wondered what $100 received a year from now is worth today if the investment promises to return 5 percent (i.e., the discount rate is 5 percent). The *present value* of that $100 is $95.24, which she determined using the following formula:

$$(($100 \, / 105\%) * 100\%)$$

Looking at it another way, $95.24 invested today at a 5 percent interest rate will be worth $100 in a year.

But present value alone was not going to solve the problem of whether to hire another salesperson. She needed to consider the initial cost of finding and hiring the employee as well. Factoring in this upfront investment would give Jen the salesperson's *net present value* (NPV). NPV is a key indication of whether a project or investment will increase the value of a business. If NPV is positive, the investment is financially attractive. If NPV is zero, the financial value of the business does not change and the investment is neutral. And if NPV is negative, the financial value of the business should decrease, rendering it an unattractive investment.

This discovery was immediately useful to Jen. She was in the initial stages of hiring a super salesperson away from the competition. This person would cost Permanent about $150,000 per year in salary plus another $25,000 in fringe benefits. Permanent would have to spend about $100,000 upfront to attract this employee. This would cover a headhunter's fee (of all things for a staffing firm to pay!) and up-fitting an office for him with furniture and computer equipment. Jen believed this employee would generate income of at least $75,000 per year in excess of his salary and benefits and that he would stay with the company for at least five years. Finally, Jen expected to earn a return of about 20 percent on her overall investment in Permanent.

Jen wondered: would hiring this employee add to the firm's value? If "yes," how much?

She sketched out the following scenario:

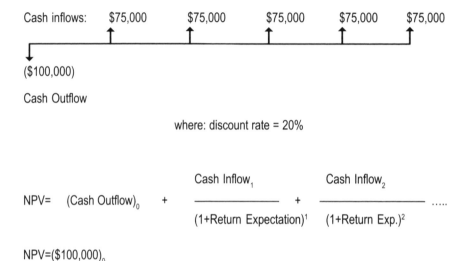

NPV Calculation

Super Salesperson Project

Cash inflows: $75,000 $75,000 $75,000 $75,000 $75,000

($100,000)

Cash Outflow

where: discount rate = 20%

$$NPV = (\text{Cash Outflow})_0 + \frac{\text{Cash Inflow}_1}{(1+\text{Return Expectation})^1} + \frac{\text{Cash Inflow}_2}{(1+\text{Return Exp.})^2} \; \ldots$$

$$NPV = (\$100,000)_0$$
$$+$$
$$\frac{\$75,000_1}{(1+20\%)^1} + \frac{\$75,000_2}{(1+20\%)^2} + \frac{\$75,000_3}{(1+20\%)^3} + \frac{\$75,000_4}{(1+20\%)^4} + \frac{\$75,000_5}{(1+20\%)^5}$$

= ($100,000)   investment in new employee

+ $224,000   present value of the five year cash flows

$124,000   net present value (as rounded)

By hiring the new salesperson, Permanent would be better off finan-cially by $124,000. In other words, the shareholders had a net present value on this investment of $124,000. Jen could use this information to negotiate with the employee. For instance, she knew that she had some room to offer him a higher salary if necessary. At the same time, if he left at the end of 18 months, the NPV of the investment in hiring him would be reduced to $4,000. To manage this risk, Jen could require he sign a two-year employ-ment agreement.

Economic Value – Another Way?

Much as she felt about the payback method, Jen was uncomfortable with net present value analysis. She didn't feel right making decisions based on things she expected to happen several years in the future. Like most business own-ers, she was a creature of optimism, and she knew instinctively that relying on her rose-colored glasses might lead to bad decision-making. Further, she wanted a financial metric that was easy to use, which NPV wasn't. So once again she went in search of answers.

This time, she found something close to what she needed: Economic Value Added (EVA). EVA is a measure that was created by the management consulting firm Stern Stewart & Co. to measure changes to shareholders' wealth, and it's mainly used by managers of large public companies. The key insight underlying EVA is similar to the logic behind NPV: Earning a return greater than the cost of capital increases value and earning less than the cost of capital decreases value.

But EVA was not really designed to help managers of small private com-panies. For instance, it assumes that managers want to maximize taxable income – something few owners have as a goal.

Evaluating Project Performance

So Jen improvised. She decided to borrow from several sources to create her own calculation, which she dubbed *economic value* (EV). Jen chose the salesperson project to help her get her mind around economic value. Using this approach, if project earnings exceed required returns from the project investment, Permanent creates positive economic value (in other words, positive value for the shareholders), and vice versa.

First, she focused on return. As shown above, hiring the salesperson should add $75,000 per year in profits. Project investment, or the cost of hiring the salesperson, was approximately $100,000. An owner could expect to receive about five times recast earnings in a sale for a staffing company like Permanent. Thus, the market viewed Permanent's risk at about 20 percent (the reciprocal of five is one-fifth, or 20 percent). Jen thought this was a fair risk assessment.

Jen had the makings of a formula:

Economic value = Project Earnings - (Required Return * Project Investment)
            = $75,000 - (20% * $100,000)
            = $75,000 - $20,000
            = $55,000

Hiring a new salesperson would increase the value of Permanent by $55,000. This is less than the $124,000 that NPV indicated it would add, but both methods said that bringing him on board would increase the value of the company. Furthermore, the two methods gave almost the identical answer when Jen looked only three years into the future. But unlike NPV, economic value was easy to calculate and there was no need for a crystal ball.

So Jen had her answer: Buy. She "bought" a talented new salesperson, and she bought into the notion that better financial decision-making was a critical element of increasing the value of her business.

BLUEPRINT

The world of economic value is separate and distinct from all other value worlds. Years ago, EV was known as residual income analysis, and later, return on net assets. Although it relies on numbers from financial statements, it jettisons many of the accounting field's definitions of value, such as book value. And the EV world generates an incremental value calculus as opposed to absolute values derived in the other value worlds. For example, if a company generates a positive economic value of $1 million, this means the company has bettered the shareholders' position by $1 million, not that the company is worth $1 million.

Economic value is defined as generating revenues beyond the corresponding economic costs. Remember what Drucker said, which I quoted in Chapter 1: "Until a business returns a profit that is greater than its cost of capital, it operates at a loss. Until then it does not create wealth; it destroys it." Indeed, if managers don't consider cost of capital when making investment decisions, they risk destroying economic value. They should always match the cost of capital with the risk and return of the potential investment, and projects that are riskier should always return at a higher rate than safer projects.

Net present value came of age in the 1960s. For the first time managers could use an economic approach to determine the value of companies and specific projects.. For the next 30 years, NPV was the dominant method for valuing investments. Over the past decade or two, NPV has given way to other frameworks, largely because it is derived from future cash flows and therefore not useful for incentive systems that are based on past performance and current results.

Traditional accounting methods, such as earnings per share (EPS) or return on investment (ROI), have been used for years for evaluating strategic decisions. Over the last 10 years, a key consideration has been that economic

— not accounting — concepts drive value. The most recent economic value metrics have emphasized easily implemented calculations that can serve multiple purposes. Perhaps the best known is Economic Value Added (EVA).

Problems with Using Traditional Methods

Because accounting methods are primarily cost-oriented, as opposed to value-oriented, they are not always in alignment with the goal of wealth creation. They can tell you what is spent and even what you made, but they don't necessarily tell you if you made enough to cover your company's' cost of capital. In addition, accounting measures ignore the time value of capital invested. Each type of capital has a cost based on the return expectations of the market. The time value of debt capital is reflected in the rate of interest charged, while providers of equity capital "charge" an ownership stake in exchange for investing in your company and not another.

A company committed to maximizing shareholder returns will use value-based approaches to make decisions. For most private companies, managers are the shareholders, but as the business grows and becomes more sophisticated, it becomes increasingly important to separate the goal of creating wealth for the owners from that of creating wealth in the business.

There are a number of ways to measure economic value. The net present value method is probably the most popular because it has been around the longest, but it comes with several pitfalls. Forecasts of future cash flows tend to be overly optimistic, causing a 'hockey stick' pattern that can overvalue the project's projected returns. Also, NPV is a stock measure and not particularly useful for bonus or incentive programs. So while NPV is theoretically correct, it may not be the best value-creating approach a private company can use. EV, on the other hand, is easy to use, plus it indicates whether the project earns a return greater than the company's cost of capital.

The following steps can be taken to successfully adopt economic value as your company's decision-making metric:

1. Determine the project metrics, i.e., the total investment, likely return, and expected return to the shareholders. Total investment means all costs associated with making the investment, both hard and soft. A fixed expense such as buying a piece of equipment is a hard cost; installing and maintaining the equipment is a soft cost.

2. Determine the equity return expectation. For small companies this is typically 30-40 percent; for middle market companies, 20-30 percent; for larger companies, 10-20 percent. But since the expected return is what the ownership requires from its investment in the company, it is whatever the owners say it is. Return expectations for investments should vary based on the riskiness of the particular project. For instance, a project requiring skills outside of your company's core competencies would carry a higher risk factor than one that demands existing skill sets.

3. Use this formula to calculate economic value:

Economic value = Project Earnings - (Required Return * Project Investment)

4. Determine economic value on a routine basis for all of your financial decisions. This analysis is useful to determine if hirings, asset acquisitions, and most other major financial decisions will add to shareholder value.

Creating wealth with a business requires managers to make thousands of financial decisions over the life of their companies. Determining economic value helps them make better decisions and should be part of every owner's analytical arsenal.

21

The Value of Investment
A PRIVATE FINANCE STRATEGY

Stan Harris sat behind his desk dwelling on the past quarter-century. He had spent nearly half his life building his business, Harris & Summers, CPAs, starting with the modest goal of giving high-quality, affordable accounting help to small and mid-sized companies.

Harris & Summers had done that and more. And through the years, Stan had studied his clients, most of whom were private business owners. He had come to the conclusion that most people do not own businesses to get rich. No, most start and manage companies to control their own destiny and have a chance at a comfortable lifestyle. Stan realized early in his career as a business owner that he was different. He wanted the lavish lifestyle and substantial wealth, and he had achieved both. His secret to success was simple: He demanded a specific return from his investment in his firm and diligently managed the business to make sure that it produced it.

Harris & Summers was not a typical CPA firm. Only 30 percent of its revenues came from traditional accounting work like audits and tax filing. Over time, Stan had moved the firm into more value-added areas, namely, forensic accounting and economic damages consulting. Because they required greater sophistication, these services enabled the firm to bill higher hourly fees.

Forensic accounting, which amounted to about 35 percent of the firm's annual revenues, is a subset of accounting that looks behind the numbers, especially in cases of financial discrepancies. The firm's team of certified forensic accountants, certified fraud examiners, certified public accountants, investigators and researchers was trained to find such discrepancies and answer the who, what, when, where, why, and how. Harris & Summers would also implement systems and controls to prevent a client from being the victim of fraud again.

Economic damages appraisals accounted for the other 35 percent of the firm's revenue. Typically, these were done in connection with lawsuits alleging personal injury, wrongful death, or employment discrimination, cases which often required financial calculations to estimate lost earnings, lost income from other sources, or the value of forgone fringe benefits.

Stan knew that most accounting and consulting firms charged by the hour for nearly all assignments, and each employee had an hourly charge associated with his or her efforts. For example, senior consultants might earn $300 per hour while analysts might get $75 per hour. The problem with this approach, in Stan's opinion, was that the number of hours and the rate charged might or might not correspond to the amount of value created for the firm. For instance, if a $300-per-hour consultant needed support from a team of researchers in order to do the job, was he generating wealth for the firm?

Investment in the Conceptual Age

Stan considered this problem for many years before deciding to tie employee billing to the investment required to generate his desired return.

Managers are taught to use return-on-investment ratios to judge the effectiveness of an organization. This simple calculation divides some income number by the investment in the company, such as equity or assets.

As a CPA, Stan knew these ratios were created generations ago, back when tangible assets ruled the balance sheet. But Harris & Summers, like most companies in America today, was a service provider. It invested in people, not machines, and consequently, its assets walked out of the office each night. The firm's "book value" was only $500,000, but its real worth was obviously much greater than that.

To make return-on-investment useful, Stan came up with a definition he felt would be more appropriate for his business. Stan believed that in a service company, investment was the total amount spent on each productive employee that enabled that employee to do his or her job. This included salary, benefits, cars, travel, and other perquisites, as well as some allocation of non-productive overhead expenses, such as compensation for support staff. Harris & Summers employed 25 productive employees and five non-productive employees. Productive employees had direct client contact and generated billings while non-productive employees provided general support services such as administration, clerical work, and computer assistance.

To determine total investment, Stan first added up the annual non-productive overhead that was not attributable to an individual employee:

Harris & Summers
Nonattributable, Nonproductive Investment Analysis

Building rent	$250,000
Owner salary	250,000
Nonproductive salaries not attributable	250,000
Nonproductive insurances	50,000
Computer support	300,000
Subscriptions	150,000
Other expenses	750,000
Total Nonproductive Expenses	$2,000,000

This $2 million represented the investment the firm made in its people each year. Stan would allocate a share of that sum to each of the 25 productive employees.

Determining investment in each productive employee was fairly straightforward. Stan listed expenses that directly tied to the employee, such as salary and fringes, as well as the allocated nonproductive expenses described above. In addition, he tacked on any nonproductive investments that were directly attributable to that employee, such as support staff who worked for no one else. The following shows the investment analysis for Rick O'Brien, a senior consultant with the firm.

Harris & Summers

Productive Investment Analysis for Rick O'Brien

Rick O'Brien salary	$ 125,000
O'Brien insurances	25,000
O'Brien vehicle	5,000
O'Brien travel	35,000
Nonproductive salary and fringes*	130,000
Nonattributable investment allocated	80,000
Total O'Brien Investment	$ 400,000

*nonproductive staff charged directly to O'Brien

Rick O'Brien's direct expenses, such as salary, travel, and the cost of his indirect support staff, comprise most of the costs. Based on his salary, Rick was also charged with $80,000 of the nonattributable nonproductive investment. Looking at this, Stan determined that he could not receive any return on his investment in Rick O'Brien until Rick's billings exceeded $400,000 per year.

The Return

Of course, Stan wouldn't be satisfied with simply exceeding his costs. He figured he needed to make a return of at least 25 percent on his investment in his employees, for several reasons.

First, he truly believed that every small business was a phone call away from oblivion, thanks to lawsuits and other catastrophic events. This risk merited a high return. Second, he wanted to earn about twice what he could on investment in public equities, which at that time was about 12 percent. Finally, he knew that by exploiting niche markets, Harris and Summers should have no difficulty achieving a 25 percent return, so it wasn't an unreasonable expectation.

How would this affect Stan's employees? Returning to the example above, Rick O'Brien would need to generate $500,000 in billings each year to meet Stan Harris' minimum return expectation ($400,000 times 1.25%). This annual sum corresponded to roughly $250 per hour ($500,000 divided by 2,000 hours).

Viewing investment and return in this holistic way solved several major
problems for Stan:

- He could now determine the return-on-investment for each
  productive employee
- He could develop compensation schemes for productive employees
  around return targets
- He could determine optimum hourly billing rates for each
  productive employee
- Productive employees would have an incentive to police and
  minimize non-productive expenses
- Productive employees would become part of the marketing effort
  because they would know their "investment nut"
- Those who did not meet the return on investment goals would not
  be surprised when they were replaced
- Stan could manage his goal of meeting a certain return on his
  investment in the firm all the way down at the individual employee
  level

Over time, Harris & Summers' culture adapted to Stan's return-on-investment system. Employees began thinking of themselves as members of
"work cells" in which everyone carried his or her weight or faced consequences from the team. The firm generated a monthly profit-and-loss statement
for each productive employee, so they all knew where they stood. And now
that they knew exactly what was expected of them, they became more aggressive marketers for the firm.

Satisfying the Superstars

The cream that rose to the top of Harris & Summers warranted special treatment. Stan had five consultants who billed more than $1.5 million each year but whose total investment was less than $1 million. Stan knew that he would lose these superstars unless he shared some of the firm's upside with them. So employees generating more than $1 million in annual billings qualified for a key person bonus pool that paid them 30 percent of the difference between billings and investment. For example, a consultant who billed $1.4 million on a pre-bonus investment of $1 million received a bonus of $120,000 (($1.4 million - $1 million) * 30%).

Improving the Model

Despite these changes, Stan had never been comfortable selling just employee hours. He wanted to sell impact. To accomplish this, he converted some of his consulting areas, such as delivery of valuation reports and economic workups, to fixed-fee billing. The routine stuff was outsourced to independent contractors, many of them women CPAs who had young children at home. These women were highly qualified, could work from home, and wanted a flexible schedule. Plus, they worked for about $25 to $30 per hour, much less than a full-time CPA. The firm ultimately employed more than 25 of them, an approach that allowed the firm to bill increasing amounts of work while allowing employees to focus on more value-added assignments.

The Net Result

Back at his desk, as Stan reflected on his accomplishments, he couldn't help but smile. Harris & Summers was generating more than $15 million in annual revenues and more than $3.5 million in profits. Stan's role in the business was purely strategic: he hadn't directly worked on an audit or consulting job for more than six years. Turnover was low because everyone knew what was expected and where he or she stood. Most importantly, Stan had institutionalized a way to routinely realize the value of his firm's investments and create substantial wealth.

BLUEPRINT

It's ironic that the Midas Manager of this story, a CPA, had to get beyond traditional accounting measurement methodology to understand the nature of value in his business. Stan Harris might not have said it, but he recognized that accounting deals with costs while finance deals with values. Accounting captures information about transactions with third parties that occurred in the past, like the cost of goods sold. Historical information is necessary for running a business, but it isn't sufficient to predict what will happen in the future, especially in the Conceptual Age, in which the past is often not predictive.

As businesses increasingly adopt conceptual business models, most of the value they create will be intangible value, another weak spot in accounting. Harris & Summers, whose tangible book value was only $500,000, had a market value of more than $15 million that was based almost entirely on intangibles. Because intangibles like the ones that Stan was measuring are generated internally, not externally, their value isn't recognized in a company's financial statements.

So what is a manager to do, ignore accounting? Of course not. In this story, accounting systems are used to capture the expenses that underlie Stan's system for analyzing his investment in his employees. But the system relies on principles of finance to figure employees' intangible value and motivate them to create more of it.

Stan knew that he needed to institutionalize his system at Harris & Summers if he wanted to reduce his risk of ownership. The success of all professional practices depends on assets that walk out the door every night. Without a good method for measuring and compensating these resources, they might not be back in the morning. Creating an effective system enabled Stan to consistently generate high returns without the risk normally associated with owning a professional practice.

The following steps can be used to replicate this strategy:

1. Consider the differences between accounting and finance. Both disciplines are useful, but dividing up labor between the two is unavoidable.

2. Focus your business on niches. This enables productive employees to more effectively meet both their goals and yours.

3. Consider investment broadly, not strictly from an accounting perspective.

4. Allocate expenses fairly. In some cases, it is fine to directly allocate non-productive expenses to a productive employee, such as the cost of a dedicated work cell. Your employees will notice if they receive an unfair allocation.

5. Let productive employees carry the load. This strategy does not work if decisions such as the choice of team members are made on a top-down basis.

6. Give productive employees monthly income statements and your entire workforce twice-yearly performance reviews.

7. Give productive employees the tools they need to be successful, but make them responsible for using those tools.

8. Pay your superstars what they're worth. This strategy fails if it is designed to meet the needs of average employees.

Finally, and most importantly, stop working on day-to-day projects and start managing the system. It's the only way to get the full value out of your investments.

INVESTMENT BANKER MAN

Why it's so difficult to value a business appraiser's opinion

22

An Owner's
Perspective On Value

A PRIVATE FINANCE STRATEGY

Big Jim Putnam, as his friends called him, was big in every way — big appetite for life, big giver to charities, and a big father figure to his employees.

Over the past two decades Big Jim had built a fairly big company, too: Continental Assemblies. Continental made wire harnesses for the auto industry that made the windshield wipers, the A/C and all of a car's other electrical equipment work properly.

Big Jim had always viewed his key managers as the essential wires that made Continental work properly. As he neared retirement, he planned to do right by them and give them a chance to buy the business.

Of course, Big Jim would want a big price. He could make a strong case that Continental was a very valuable company. In fact, he figured Continental generated about $5 million of income each year, profits which he viewed as his own personal annuity:

Continental Assemblies

Income Stream

	$000
Total Compensation to Jim, including bonuses	900
+ Pretax earnings	3,600
+ Jim's personal expenses[1]	150
+ Effect of close business contracts[2]	20
+ Jim's covered expenses (insurance, business vacations, etc.)	50
+ Other items personally benefiting Jim[3]	180
Income stream to Jim	$5,000

[1]Vacations and conferences charged to Continental
[2]Excess rent charged to Continental by a company controlled by Jim
[3]Charitable donations ($150), legal fees ($20), and accounting fees ($10)

If anyone asked, Big Jim's reasoning was simple: He had started and still owned the company. Therefore, he had earned it. Of course, no one ever asked.

Jim believed that Continental could grow this $5 million cash flow for the foreseeable future. He also believed there was a low risk that it wouldn't increase. In his mind, Jim settled on a price of $50 million for the company. The only question was how to realize this price.

Big Jim was big on planning, too. For the past few months, he had obsessed about how he would transfer Continental to his managers. Finally, he told them to offer the highest price that the capital markets would support. This put the managers squarely in the world of investment value. But Big Jim had every intention of selling his business in the much more lucrative world of owner value.

Big Jim believed Continental's president, John Jenson, who had managed the company for five years, was experienced enough to own it. He also knew that, given the miserly salaries Continental paid, his managers didn't have money to buy it. But John was no fool, either. He knew that Continental was a great company. He was confident he could raise money through a combination of debt and outside equity.

While John was delighted that Big Jim had approached him to buy the business, he didn't have a clue about tapping the private markets. When in doubt, hire an expert, he thought. After hearing from an acquaintance that local investment banker Jack Womble was a good dealmaker, John hired him. John told Jack that he and two other managers could invest about $500,000 combined. Womble thought to himself that this was a record high amount for managers to invest in a buyout. Management teams never brought much money to the table.

As a starting point, Jack reviewed Continental's balance sheet. After some study and quick calculations, he determined the company's margined collateral value, which was the amount a senior lender would loan his clients:

Continental Assemblies
Collateral Value

($000)

Asset Class	Stated Value	Lendable Value/ Fair Market Value	Advance Rate	Margined Collateral Value
Accounts Receivable	$3,000	2,750	80%	$2,200
Inventory	2,000	1,500	40%	600
Land/Buildings	2,500	3,500	70%	2,450
Machinery & Eqpt.	1,500	1,000	65%	650
Total				$6,000

The 'Stated Value' for each of the asset classes came off of Continental's balance sheet. The 'Lendable Value/Fair Market Value' was the amount eligible for secured lending (after eliminating past due invoices, related-company invoices and other ineligible receivables and work-in-progress inventory and reducing buildings and machinery and equipment to their fair market values). Applying an advance rate to the eligible assets generated a margined collateral value, which for Continental totaled about $6 million. Jack told John he would choose the lender with the best combination of advance rates and loan costs.

Jack quietly thanked his lucky stars that he took this assignment on an hourly basis (plus success fee). To him, $6 million did not represent very much borrowing power. He would need some luck in the mezzanine market. Jack contacted his golfing buddy, Tim, at American Mezzanine Capital, and gave him the numbers on Continental:

Continental Summary Financials

Book Value		$4.0 million
Benefit Stream		
Pretax Earnings	$3.6 million	
Prior Owner Compensation	9 million	
Prior Owner Discretionary Expenses	4 million	
Depreciation	.7 million	
Normalized Capital Expenditures	(.4) million	
Adjusted EBITDA		$5.2 million

Expected Stream growth in next 5 years: 15%	$10.5 million in Year 5
Projected CASH at end of 5th Year	$20.0 million

Tim reviewed this information, along with the reams of background on Continental that John had created but Jack now claimed as his own.

Somewhere deep in the bowels of American Mezzanine Capital prowled an algorithm that determined how much the firm could contribute to the Continental buyout. It would not lend more than two-and-a-half times Continental's adjusted EBITDA, or about $13 million. Tim believed the company could afford a healthy interest payment, and its projected cash balance of $20 million at the end of the fifth year would be more than enough to pay off a loan of that size.

But Tim's term sheet would have choked a whale. There was a 12 percent coupon payable quarterly and a warrant on 10 percent of Continental's stock that could be exercised starting in Year 4. The firm had valued the warrants using a formula in which the price increased over time, which would entice John and his team to buy them back as soon as possible. Based on Jack's expectation that Continental would be worth at least $60 million in Year 5 ($10 million EBITDA times a six multiple), the warrants had a value of at least $6 million. Continental could buy them back and be debt free with a strong earnings base at the end of Year 5.

But Jack slyly acted the part of an insulted broker aghast at such harsh terms. In reality, he was thrilled to have commitments for almost $20 million in all ($500,000 management investment plus $6 million asset-based loan plus $13 million mezzanine loan). The last stop was the world of private equity.

Jack told John he thought they could raise $10 million in private equity. That sounded good, but John quickly realized he and the other two managers had a math problem. If they took an outside investment of $10 million, their $500,000 would merit only 5 percent of the equity in Continental after the deal closed ($500,000 divided by $10 million). For the first time, it occurred to John that he might be better off working for Big Jim and owning no stock than investing all of his money to split such a miniscule stake.

But wait! Jack was about to earn his fee. He told John that he knew a private equity group, U.S. Equity, that specialized in backing management teams and giving extra credit to their investments. In other words, it offered them stakes in their companies that were bigger than what their pro rata share would have been. After several meetings and two rounds of golf, the partners at U.S. Equity offered to cut John and his team in for 10 percent of the equity in Continental. If they hit financial targets, the managers could *earn-in* another 2 percent per year over five years, upping their stake to as high as 20 percent.

The offer was the result of a fairly disciplined approach. Typical for a private equity group (PEG), U.S. Equity expected a 30 percent return on its investments. The firm believed Continental would be debt-free in Year 5 and earning about $10 million per year at that time. At seven times EBITDA, the company could sell for $70 million. If John and his team hit all of its bogeys, U.S. Equity's stake would be 80 percent, or about $56 million. Was this enough to warrant a $10 million investment today? A financial calculator gave the answer: the compounded return would be about 40 percent, meaning U.S. Equity was good to go.

John was not, however. He refused to play unless he could own at least 35 percent of Continental, and his fellow managers each needed at least 10 percent. He was not in this deal to work for someone else. But John's demand for a 55 percent management stake caused an uproar at U.S. Equity. To begin with, it was a control player. Furthermore, a 45 percent stake would generate at most a 25 percent return on its $10 million investment. U.S. Equity was not playing this game.

Big Jim had watched all of this from the sidelines. He wasn't surprised when John came to him with his dilemma: he and the other two managers had only $19.5 million committed to fund a buyout of Continental. He didn't explain it in these terms, but $19.5 million was the investment value his team had put on the company. It was the most they could reasonably raise in the capital markets and still meet their expectations.

But Big Jim had already made up his mind that he would transfer the company in the world of owner value. The issue was how best to do it, and now was the time to decide. He didn't want to take a seller note that would leave him in third-lien position behind the asset-based lender and the mezzanine guys. That was taking equity risk for a lender's return, which made no sense.

So Big Jim proposed something unexpected. He would sell John and the other two managers 65 percent of Continental stock for $19.5 million. He would keep the rest but protect his minority interests. Big Jim would never personally guarantee any of the company's debts, he would take $20,000 per month in management fees, and he would insist on a shareholder agreement that would shelter him from anti-dilution and other events that could be harmful to his interests.

Finally, he would hold a put option allowing him to sell his shares back to the managers as soon as they retired the mezzanine debt. Here was the formula he used to value the option:

Big Jim's Shares = (Continental recast EBITDA for most recent fiscal year * 7 * 35%)

Big Jim believed that Continental's recast EBITDA in the sixth year would be about $12 million, thus he would receive about $29 million for his shares when he exercised his put option.

More importantly, Big Jim thought that he understood the risk of partnering with his managers. He had recruited them and trained them to run his business, and they had his full confidence. He felt good about making a deal with them.

From the outset, Big Jim Putnam believed his company was worth about $50 million. As it turned out, it was worth even more. All told, he received $55 million for Continental Assemblies: $20 million at the closing; $1.4 million in management fees over seven years; and $33 million when he exercised the option to sell his remaining shares and retired for good. As usual, Big Jim took his big paydays in stride. He couldn't imagine it turning out any other way, and no one else could either.

BLUEPRINT

What lessons can be learned from this management buyout? First, managers need to manage. Leave the heavy deal-making to a professional. A common issue in management transfers is that the managers *work for* the owner. They can't have nose-to-nose negotiations with their employer. John was smart to hire an investment banker. If the deal had failed, he and Big Jim could have blamed the dealmaker and walked away from the negotiating table with their relationship intact.

Second, the dealmaker should engineer a funding solution that considers the entire capital structure. All capital sources have credit boxes that describe the characteristics required of borrowers seeking funding. This knowledge enables dealmakers to plan capital access.

Once a plan is in place, each capital provider issues a term sheet outlining the terms of the proposed financing. The battle is won or lost at this point. A good dealmaker conducts this symphony of interests with a careful baton. Dealmakers also need to incorporate the full capital structure with all of its layers into their detailed projections. This requires a thorough understanding of effective returns for each source of capital. Finally, the management team should sign the letter of intent with the owner and then shop the deal to a number of equity sources. Once again, the equity split and ownership term sheets are negotiated together.

The following steps can be taken by owners to convert a business from the world of investment value to the world of owner value:

1. Understand the difference between investment and owner value. Investment value is the value to a specific investor based on his or her unique return expectation. In the case of Continental Assemblies, the investor

was the management team. Management teams are typically constrained as to the amount of capital they can raise to support investment value.

2. If you want to sell your business in the owner value world — and most owners do because it generates values that make sense to them — you have to be willing to participate in the risk of the deal.

3. Let the investor establish the highest investment value possible before moving the deal into the world of owner value. This will give you a full view into the valuation and capitalization process the investor has undertaken.

4. Carefully gauge the risk of converting a deal to the world of owner value. Sometimes the investor is an outside buyer, which can add to the risk profile. In such a case, satisfy yourself with the cash you receive at closing and think of any subsequent payouts as gravy.

5. Convert the deal to owner value. The most straightforward way to do this is to loan the investor the money in the form of a seller note. While this is simple, it also puts you in a second- or third-lien position, which might be too risky if you are receiving a lender's rate of return.

   Another option is an earn-out, which is a method for triggering changes in the purchase price based on the future performance of the company. An earn-out is a bridge tool to help buyers and sellers reach an agreement, but it can be dangerous. It is extremely hard to structure an earn-out to take the intent of both parties into account. Before agreeing to one, hire an expert in this area. As with seller notes, you should be satisfied with the closing proceeds when an earn-out is involved.

   Big Jim chose a put option, which allowed him to participate in the risk and return of the deal. This is a good choice when a large upside exists, but it helps to take out some compensation along the way, such as a management fee. You can also use a warrant, which is explained in Chapter 8, or a warrant in combination with a seller loan.

6. Structure the deal to retain effective control of your investment even though legal control has been transferred. Giving up control is particularly difficult for owners who have spent their careers with a tight grip on it. Shareholder agreements protect your minority rights, or at the very least, your financial position.

Not all owners are ultimately able to sell their companies in the world of owner value. Most business transfers occur in the worlds of market value or fair market value. But if you understand private finance, you're willing to plan, and you don't mind taking on some risk, you can get what you want, whether you're big or small.

INVESTMENT BANKER MAN

IB Man: Able to leap tall valuations with a single recast

23

Sharing the Wealth

A PRIVATE FINANCE STRATEGY

As they neared the big six-oh, Steve Torres and his wife Diane felt good that they had met four of their five goals as business owners.

After nearly 25 years with Steve at the helm and Diane running the office, sales at Torres Distribution (TDI) had surpassed $50 million a year. Their company was now a major regional supplier of plumbing products. They had given their son, Tyler, a great education. And they had welcomed him into the family business, where over 10 years he had risen to the position of general manager.

Now Steve, who started in the industry as a shipping clerk, hatched a plan to achieve the final goal: make himself, his wife, and his son financially independent for life. Like most American business owners, Steve loved his country but hated paying more than his fair share of taxes, so his plan had to include a smart tax strategy. More importantly, his plan had to allow him to plan in the world of fair market value and sell in the much richer world of market value.

Fair Market Value

The first step of Steve's plan was to establish a fair market value for Torres Distribution. Steve planned to give 30 percent of the company's stock to his son, and stock gifts are valued in the fair market value world. Why? Because the U.S. government says so. More specifically, because the Internal Revenue Service says so.

The year before, Steve had attended an estate planning seminar during which the speaker had described the world of fair market value. It was a confusing talk. Steve remembered only some key terms: Hypothetical values, willing buyer and seller, discounting. None of what he recalled seemed to make sense. Steve wasn't even sure if fair market values were intended to reflect reality.

Steve needed an outside expert. He called appraiser Danny Stevens to determine the fair market value of a 30 percent interest in TDI. Danny told Steve that he would follow a U.S. Treasury Ruling issued in 1959 that is still the authority fair market valuations. But, he said, there were a variety of factors that appraisers must consider when determining fair market value. Minority interests could be discounted substantially due to their inability to control the strategic decisions and finances of the company, sometimes by more than 50 percent. A lack of marketability discount of 20 to 40 percent could also be applied when comparing private companies, which have no ready market for selling their stock, to public ones.

After briefing his customer, Danny turned to appraising TDI. To arrive at an unadjusted indicated value, that is, the company's total worth before discounts, Danny multiplied its net income of $1 million by eight, the multiple at which comparable public companies were trading at the time. Next, to figure the basis for calculating a 30 percent share, Danny applied a 25 percent minority interest discount and a 25 percent discount for lack of marketability (DLOM). Note that, according to IRS rules, discounts must be applied subsequently, i.e., the minority interest discount is applied first and the DLOM second:

Application of Adjustments

Torres Distribution Unadjusted Indicated Value:	$8,000,000
(value on a controlling, marketable basis)	
Less minority discount (25%)	2,000,000
Value on a minority, marketable basis	$6,000,000
Less DLOM (25%)	1,500,000
Torres Distribution Adjusted Indicated Value	$4,500,000

The discounts freed Steve and Diane to pass along more stock to their son tax-free. The IRS allowed each of them an "exemption equivalent," which is the right to transfer $1 million worth of assets without incurring gift or estate taxes. At TDI's adjusted value of $4,500,000, Tyler's 30 percent of the stock would be worth $1,350,000. By making the gift in the world of fair market value, Steve and Diane avoided writing a hefty check to Uncle Sam.

Market Value

Steve waited almost a year before launching phase two of his plan. He had been watching as two different companies consolidated many of his competitors in the plumbing supply business. He could foresee a time when Torres Distribution would be at a disadvantage due to its smaller size. The time was ripe to attempt a transfer at market value.

Steve hired investment banker Tim Golder, a seasoned pro, to sell the company. He explained that his firm would run a private auction with only synergistic buyers invited:

Private Auction: Steps to Completion

Execute a Confidentiality Agreement

⇩

Distribute a Selling Memorandum

⇩

Buyer Visits

⇩

Call for Offers

⇩

Negotiate Synergy Sharing

⇩

Execute a Letter of Intent

⇩

Buyer Due Diligence / Definitive Agreements

⇩

Closing

Tim sent a fact sheet and confidentiality agreement, neither of which named Torres Distribution, to 10 prospective buyers. Of the seven that responded, two were eliminated after Tim learned more about their acquisition programs. The five remaining received a Selling Memorandum, which included a recast income statement for TDI:

Torres Distribution
Recast Income Statement

Item	Y/E 20X3	Y/E 20X2	Y/E 20X1
Operating Profits	$1,400	$1,590	$1,650
Adjustments			
Depreciation	356	360	358
Excess Owner Comp[1]	150	50	0
Management Fees[2]	200	189	304
Interest[3]	35	49	54
Officer Insurance[4]	5.0	4.5	4.6
Excess Accounting[5]	6.5	10.5	8.5
Excess Legal[6]	9.9	9.6	12
Excess Rent[7]	8.7	0	0
Excess Health Insur.	8.2	14	14
Casualty Loss - fire[8]	35	0	0
One-time Consulting[9]	0	55	0
Charitable Donations[10]	74	69	72
Employee Incentives[11]	125	115	117
Total Adjustments	1,013	926	944
Recast EBITDA	**$2,413**	**$2,516**	**$2,594**

[1]Majority owner's compensation added back
[2]Annual management fees paid to company controlled by majority owner
[3]Interest expense added back to accurately depict cash flow
[4]Majority owner's officer insurance added back
[5]Fees for accounting services performed mainly for another company the majority owner controls
[6]Judgment against former employee accused of theft (one-time expense)
[7]Assumes new owner will not continue paying current rent
[U] Uninsured portion of damage due to fire (one-time expense)
[9]A consultant was hired to perform design studies for a new product, which was not produced
[10]Company gives donations each year to a charity supported by majority owner
[11]Includes bonuses that only a passive shareholder would institute

No price was set, but Tim believed prospective buyers would "buy into" recast EBITDA of about $2.5 million. He also believed they would view the risk of TDI hitting its earnings targets at about 20 percent, since recent acquisitions in the industry had been going for about five times recast earnings. Multiplying the likely recast EBITDA by the likely selling multiple yielded a likely enterprise value of $12.5 million, assuming the shareholders paid off TDI's long-term debt of $500,000 at closing.

Four companies decided to visit. Separately, they each met Steve, Diane, and Tyler at Tim's office over the next two weeks, and three of them visited TDI's facility at night (the other assumed correctly that there were few secrets in the plumbing supply business). Several weeks later, term sheets for three different offers arrived. One was for $13.75 million and the other two were for less than $12 million apiece. One prospective buyer had decided against making an offer.

It was Show Time for Tim. The high bid had come from a company in the industry that could horizontally integrate TDI into their own operation. In five cities, TDI had branches basically right next to its own, each carrying $300,000 in annual costs ($150,000 in rent; $65,000 in manager salary; $75,000 in other salaries; $10,000 other). The buyer could shut the TDI branches down and save about $1.5 million a year. Tim believed the buyer would give him credit for about 30 percent of the total synergies, or $500,000, increasing TDI's income stream to about $3 million a year.

After another month of hard fighting, Tim had upped the bid to $16.5 million:

Original Offer: **$13.75 million**

Original Multiple Offered: @5.5 times recast EBITDA

Original recast EBITDA $2.5 million

Ultimate Offer: **$16.5 million**

Ultimate Multiple Offered: @5.5 times recast EBITDA + shared synergies

Ultimate Income Stream $3 million ($2.5 MM EBITDA + $.5 MM Synergy)

Steve and Diane said yes, paid off $500,000 in long-term debt, and achieved their goal of financial independence for their family for life.

Tyler received $3.6 million at the closing ($16 million times 30 percent less 25% taxes due on the sale) in addition to a three-year employment agreement paying as much as $350,000 per year. And he was only 33 years old.

His parents retired $8.4 million richer ($16 million times 70% less 25% taxes due on the sale). Steve and Diane celebrated by buying an oceanfront condo and traveling the world. They had achieved their final goal, financial freedom, and it felt like a dream had come true. But this dream wouldn't have been possible without a lot of hard work – and by planning in one value world and selling in another.

BLUEPRINT

Planning in the fair market value world and selling in the market value world is an option for most business owners. But executing this strategy requires a lead time of at least a couple of years. You can't rush proper planning.

Before doing anything, owners need to understand each value world fully. The fair market value world is appropriate for many tax and legal situations such as estate planning and gift-giving. The IRS is the main authority in this world and it gives appraisers guidance on performing valuations. But fair market values rarely match owners' ideas of value. That's because both are merely notional values, and in this world, value is seen from the perspective of a hypothetical willing buyer and seller, not the owner.

The world of market value is much different. Market values are based on hypothetical unwilling buyers and sellers. Typically, real-world deals are struck when both parties are equally miserable with the purchase price. Neither party is particularly happy about what the other side is offering, but neither is sufficiently unhappy to walk away from the deal. Also, like all business valuation, market value is a *range* concept. Every company has at least three market values at the same time. These are determined in subworlds and they represent the most likely selling price based on the most likely buyer type, either Asset, Financial, or Synergy.

In the Asset subworld, the most likely buyer is not interested in the company's earnings stream but rather its assets. Therefore, the most likely selling price is based on the company's net asset value, and the seller gets no credit for the company's operations or its goodwill (beyond the possible write-up of the assets).

Values in the Financial subworld reflect what an individual or non-strategic buyer would pay for the business. For either, it is based solely on the company's financial statements.

The Synergy subworld bases valuations on the market value of the company when synergies from the acquisition are considered, i.e., the expected increase in performance over what the two firms accomplish independently.

A deal really starts once the first offer is received. The first offers are typically disappointing unless one buyers tries to pre-empt the rest with a high bid. While pre-emptive offers occur too often to be considered urban myths, most of the time the intermediary takes one of several less-than-acceptable offers and attempts to improve on it. Every dealmaker has a method for doing this. One is to try to intimidate a buyer into paying more, which works better in the movies than in real life. A better approach is to try to elicit how much a buyer can afford to pay while still meeting return expectations and then propose a way for the buyer to do so, such as by sharing a portion of the anticipated synergies.

From a valuation viewpoint, synergies are typically reflected in expected increases in the income stream of the combined firm:

Synergy subworld stream = Recast EBITDA + Credited Synergies

Earnings are measured on a pretax basis since the tax status of either party typically doesn't matter in the world of market value. Many private companies are flow-through entities that pay no taxes, such as S corporations and limited liability companies. Furthermore, determining the tax rates that other parties pay is next-to-impossible given the nuances in IRS rules. Pretax earnings allow everyone to see the business from the same perspective.

Investment bankers and other intermediaries typically try to maximize synergy sharing on behalf of their clients using the private auction process. But the intermediary can influence only the numerator of the value equation, the income stream. The buyer brings the denominator, the rate of return needed to compensate for the risk of the investment:

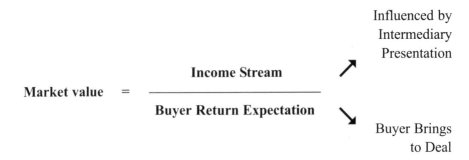

The following steps can be used to implement this strategy:

1. Before attempting this strategy, make sure the market will be receptive when you're ready to sell your company. Not every company can be transferred in the Synergy sub-world of market value. This strategy works in the Financial subworld, too, but you need to find out from brokers or investment bankers who are knowledgeable about your industry if either is an option at the outset.

2. Once it's clear you can sell your business for a pretty penny, discuss the plan with a qualified estate planner. There are numerous permutations to this strategy, so you'll need an expert from the word go.

3. Hire a certified business appraiser to perform the fair market valuation. There are more than 5,000 of them in the U.S. These people are trained in this field and have demonstrated competence. Your estate planner can help you determine what percentage of the company should be appraised based on your goals.

4. Once the appraisal is complete, give the shares to the recipient(s) named in your plan. These do not have to be family members. You can gift shares to anyone you like, even an institution.

5. Once you've made the gift, begin preparing your business for sale. Engage an investment banker to perform a pre-sale planning study. There are many things you can do to fetch a higher price for your company (see Chapter 7). Nothing beats the presence of aggressive buyers in the market, though. A good investment banker can help time your sale for maximum gain.

6. When you're ready to sell, your investment banker will probably run a private auction. This typically takes three to six months. If all goes well, your company will be priced in the Synergy subworld of market value.

7. Stay with the company during the transition period (two years is common) or train a manager to replace you.

Planning in one value world and then selling in another is a sophisticated strategy. It requires serious forethought and vision. Midas Managers like Steve Torres are planning fanatics. Are you?

INVESTMENT BANKER MAN

Human Translation: Their machines are ancient
and their business model is broken

24

Go Public Young Man

A PRIVATE FINANCE STRATEGY

Many private business owners dream that their companies will one day go public, and Tommy North was no different. He even fantasized about ringing the opening bell at the New York Stock Exchange and being interviewed on CNBC on the day of the big initial public offering (IPO).

Daydreams notwithstanding, this had not been an easy decision for Tommy. Not only is it extremely expensive to go public, but Sarbanes-Oxley and other regulations make running a public company both costly and time-consuming. But in the end Tommy felt he had no choice. His company, Northern Filtration, needed large amounts of capital, and the private markets could not provide it at a low-enough cost.

Northern Filtration owned a family of patents that protected its reputation as the world's foremost desalinization specialist. Tommy had stumbled onto the core technology while researching water chemistry and, backed by a venture capital firm, he left his university teaching post to commercialize it. After a successful pilot project, Northern built its first facility in the Middle East. Several years later, after a few more installations and a couple of small acquisitions, Northern had annual revenues of about $100 million and income of almost $25 million.

Fortunately for Tommy, his venture backer had lots of experience building companies and shepherding them through the IPO process. Well before Northern's revenues could justify it, the firm had helped Tommy put in place a seasoned, highly paid management team with substantial capacity for growth. Northern was designed to be a large company, and it would take talented managers to make it happen, he was told.

The IPO Team

There was another team to consider, though. An IPO's success depends on selecting and assembling the right team of professionals to handle the process of going public:

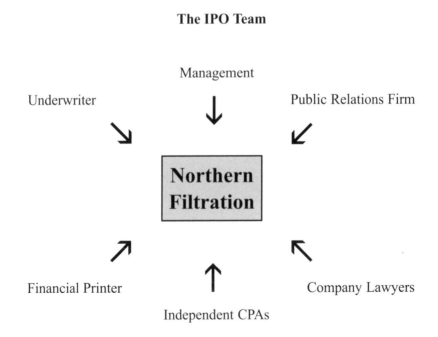

The IPO Team

Tommy and his key managers had to be fully engaged. Another key difference between a success and failure with an IPO is management's commitment to the process. Just feeding the rest of the IPO team information would be a full-time job for them.

Hiring the investment banker to underwrite and market the offering was the first step to forming the IPO team, and the venture capitalists took the lead in this effort. They understood that selecting an underwriter with the ability to distribute stock to large institutions or individual investors was crucial. But it was even more important that this firm have analysts that followed Northern's industry and would follow its stock in the future. Further, the bankers needed to offer other services, such as debt placement and merger and acquisitions advice.

The selection process had actually been initiated two years before. Northern developed relationships with several investment banking firms and selected one to lead the offering that had demonstrated the greatest commitment to its space.

As part of the selection process, each banking firm valued Northern as a public company. Tommy was amazed at the difference between his company's private and public price: In the private markets, Northern was worth about $250 million ($25 million earnings times 10); as a public entity, it was worth closer to $1 billion ($25 million times 40). Since Tommy owned 30 percent, he stood to increase his net worth on paper by more than $200 million.

Northern required the banker to take the offering on a *firm commitment* basis. That meant that the underwriter agreed to buy all of the stock that was issued and thereby assumed the risk for any unsold securities. Tommy like this approach much better than a *best efforts* offering, which had a "hope-for-the-best" feel to it. The commitment was not made until the exact offering price was negotiated, which happened just prior to the effective date of the offering. This enabled the IPO team to align the price with current market conditions.

The IPO Process

Each step of the initial public offering process involves a tremendous amount
of detail. Take a look at the complex series of steps that Tommy and Northern
had to follow:

1. Organizational Meeting

The IPO process kicked off with an organizational meeting of all of the
various parties involved in the transaction. The agenda included a discussion of the timetable for the offering, the general terms of the offering,
and the responsibilities of each member of the IPO team.

2. Registration Statement

Following the organizational meeting, Northern's lawyers began draft-
ing the *Registration Statement*. This document would be the official
prospectus for the company and ultimately would be submitted to the
Securities & Exchange Commission (SEC). Tommy appreciated that it
was required to be written in "plain English."

3. Due Diligence Matters

The due diligence process included a review of existing agreements to
determine whether any security holders had pre-emptive or registration
rights that might be triggered by the IPO. Northern's venture investor
held such rights but agreed to waive them. In addition, the company's
counsel reviewed all other agreements that might affect the offering.

4. Initial Filing

Northern filed its Registration Statement via EDGAR, the SEC web site, and issued a press release that day. The initial SEC review typically took 30 to 40 days. At the end of the review period, the agency issued a *Comment Letter* containing both legal and accounting feedback on the Registration Statement.

5. The Quiet Period

The filing of the Registration Statement commenced a *quiet period* that continued until the Registration Statement was declared effective by the SEC. During this time, representatives of the company were prohibited from providing any information about American that was not included in the Registration Statement.

6. Road Show

Once the preliminary prospectus was printed and distributed, Tommy, his chief financial officer, and his investment bankers embarked on a *road show* to major U.S. cities to market the offering to institutional investors. Nothing could have prepared Tommy for this multi-week marathon, during which he had to be on stage and on message for 15 to 20 days straight. At the end of the road show, Northern priced its IPO at $10 per share, the last step before going public.

7. Closing

Finally, Northern closed the deal. Its IPO sold 20 million shares, or about 20 percent of its total stock. Since the company was listed on NASDAQ, Tommy didn't fulfill his dream of ringing the opening bell at the NYSE, but his company did get a mention on CNBC.

From start to finish, Northern's IPO odyssey lasted nearly nine months. To Tommy, the cost was staggering: About $15 million out of $200 million the IPO raised disappeared into the pockets of the investment bankers, lawyers, and other outside players. But by selling only a minority interest to the public, Tommy and his backer still controlled the company. More importantly, Northern got the capital it needed to grow to the next level.

In less than 10 years, Tommy had taken a concept and converted it into a public entity. He had fulfilled his dream of playing in the same sandbox as Microsoft, Dell, and Google. And he had increased his personal wealth, on paper at least, by several hundred million dollars. Going public isn't for everyone, but it sure was the right direction for Tommy North.

BLUEPRINT

Out of nearly 10 million companies in the United States, only 14,000 are publicly held. Yet going public is the dream of many private business owners. It is a little like the dream of the sandlot player who is convinced he will one day make the major leagues.

There are a number of good reasons to go public, most notably to raise capital for operational expansion. Other motivations include a need for a currency with which to make acquisitions, a need to diversify and/or liquefy personal holdings, or a desire to burnish a company's reputation. Yet there are equally good reasons why a company should remain private, including the intrusion of public shareholders into the company's affairs, the market's demand for short-term financial results, the high costs of completing an IPO, and the likelihood that the owners have unrealistic expectations about the benefits of going public.

This last point is especially important and often misunderstood. Most public companies do not enjoy all the benefits of public ownership. For instance, until a public company has a *float* — the market value of its outstanding public shares — of more than $300 million, its stock will be thinly traded and its access to public capital limited. Since most companies sell only 20 percent or so of their shares at the outset, that means they have to achieve a market value of more than $1 billion just to realize one of the main reasons for doing the IPO in the first place. Thousands of public companies fall into the "should-be-private" category, and for the foreseeable future, more public companies in the U.S. will go private than the other way around.

Going public is a monumental decision with many related issues to consider, not the least of which is the owner's motivation. Simply put, unless the company has specific goals that it can't achieve as a private entity, it should not go public. A few more points to consider:

- The Exchange Matters: Most public companies are not listed on a national exchange like the NYSE or NASDAQ. Instead, their shares are traded on a minor exchange or over the counter. These *small-cap stocks* are often caught in financial purgatory. They perform well but not so well that they get the attention of the broader market, and their owners often regret going public.

- Shared Vision: Before a company goes public, the entire management team must share a corporate vision. This can't be one person's vision. Meeting the demands of the public markets requires the management depth to handle new responsibilities and new challenges. In fact, making the leap from private company boss to public company executive is one of the more difficult metamorphoses in the business world.

- Earnings Growth: To be successful as a public company requires not just a track record of high earnings growth, but also an outlook that the growth will continue. The stock market punishes companies that fail to meet their forecast or generate average, slow, or no profit growth.

- Market Timing: The market for IPOs runs in cycles. In a down period, a company that is going public can have a difficult time achieving a good price for its shares. In such cases, it is typically better to delay the offering until the market is more receptive.

• Benefits vs. Costs: Before launching an IPO, owners must ask themselves if the benefits of being a public entity outweigh the costs of achieving this status. Unless there is a clear-cut answer to this question, their company is probably better off staying private.

The decision to go public should not be made in isolation. Fortunately, there are thousands of lawyers and investment bankers who can assist in this process of corporate self-discovery.

The following steps can be followed to go public:

1. Decide whether your company and its managers can be successful in a public setting. For public companies, the spotlight is always on, and most management teams are not ready for this level of scrutiny. And make sure your company's market cap will be high enough that a minority stake offered in an IPO will be valued at least $300 million.

2. Decide how you're going to go public. An IPO is not the only way. In a *reverse merger*, a private company simply merges with one that is already publicly-held, saving the time and expense involved with organizing and marketing an offering.

3. Overbuild your management team. In the public markets, investors expect companies to have experience, credentials, and depth at the executive level.

4. Curry favor with major investment banks. It may take several years to build these relationships, but the right underwriter can make the difference between an IPO's success and failure.

5. Hang on for the ride of your life.

As the private capital markets have matured, fewer companies have felt the need to go public. At the same time, Sarbanes-Oxley and other regulatory burdens have made it prohibitively expensive for many companies to remain public. But for owners with the fortitude and the foresight to do it right, there is no substitute for the wealth that an IPO can create.

Part V

CONCLUSION

INVESTMENT BANKER MAN

Mommas, don't let your babies grow up to be arbitrageurs

25

The Nucor Way

When he was just 39, Ken Iverson became president of Nuclear Corp. of America. Instead of celebrating this promotion, Ken focused on the task at hand: making something out of a bankrupt company.

Changing the name of the company to Nucor Steel was just the beginning; Ken got busy imprinting his belief system on the struggling business. He valued intellectual curiosity and considered making mistakes as an unavoidable by-product of making things happen. He was brought up to believe that everyone had something to say and offer. Ken in particular respected people who worked with their hands just as much as those who worked with their heads. These were Ken's values, and they would be Nucor's values, too.

Engineering Value

Ken was a natural engineer with a lifelong love of machinery and making things work. He studied engineering in college, joined the Navy, and ultimately earned a master's degree in metallurgy. Then he began a series of jobs in which he built a variety of skill sets – from research and operations to sales. By the time Ken was hired to manage Nuclear's Vulcraft division, which manufactured steel joists, he had the education, experience, and drive to create value.

Unfortunately, creating value was a foreign concept at Nuclear, a mammoth company with a history of mediocrity. Founded by Ransom Olds to manufacture the REO automobile, Nuclear went bankrupt in the 1930s. It reorganized and became a profitable defense contractor during World War II, only to file for bankruptcy again after the war. During the 1960s, a New York investment banker turned the company into a conglomerate with operations in nuclear instruments, contracting, leasing, and steel joists, but most of the operations proved to be losers. By 1965, only one of Nuclear's eight divisions was profitable.

Fortunately for the owners of Nuclear, and probably unwittingly, they had promoted a Midas Manager to run the company. Ken immediately cut costs by reducing corporate staff and moving the headquarters from Phoenix to Charlotte, using just two vans to haul the entire office across the country. He chose Charlotte because it was the largest city closest to Vulcraft, the footer that would form the foundation of Nucor Steel. Once in Charlotte, Ken focused the company on becoming the low-cost joist supplier. He sold off or shuttered unprofitable divisions and put new facilities in rural areas where unions didn't exist and the agrarian work ethic was still alive.

But these moves were not enough to meet his goals, so Ken decided to backward integrate into steel production. No one would have guessed it at the time, but this decision would forever change the steel industry.

Values

Ken viewed business through a down-to-earth lens. He intuitively simplified complicated structures and processes to their most basic terms, much like one would tackle an algebraic equation. Thus, the principles underlying Nucor had to be simple and straightforward:

1. Make everyone a decision-maker
2. Minimize the layers
3. Treat people as equals
4. Encourage innovation

These principles formed the basis for the company's new strategic direction.

Everyone is a Decision-Maker

Ken believed that an employee's freedom to innovate was directly proportional to his or her distance from the corporate headquarters. With this in mind, he decentralized Nucor's operations to an exaggerated extent. Plant managers were autonomous to the point of choosing their own systems, policies, and procedures. They in turn relied on plant workers to make many of the important decisions in the company. Ken believed this "bottom-up" approach was the only way to tap into the largest pool of intellectual capital in the company — the minds of the people who actually did the work.

Workers' decisions drove the business. Nucor had no R&D department, relying instead on ideas about machinery and technology that emanated from the plant floor. This was true even for construction of new facilities. Rather than hire outside engineering and architecture firms to develop plans for a $300 million plant, Ken had Nucor workers come up with the designs and oversee construction, often on the fly. While unconventional, this enabled Nucor to construct new plants both faster and at less cost than its competitors. And there were no reprisals for making the wrong decision. Ken believed that if his employees didn't feel that they could make a mistake, they would never make a decision. This was the secret to getting workers to take ownership of the workplace.

Of course, there had to be financial incentives, too. Ken believed two questions were of fundamental import to hourly workers: 1) What am I going to be paid? and 2) Am I going to have a job tomorrow? So he developed a bonus plan that provided answers for both while raising the level of labor productivity to the point where Nucor could undercut the competition. Unlike traditional systems, Nucor's bonus plan promoted teamwork and a feeling of long-term loyalty to the company. Moreover, all employees were included in the system, including Ken.

For production workers, the basic incentive was a weekly bonus tied to measurable output. Teams of 25 to 30 employees first had to meet a target of 90 percent of the output historically produced during a full week of work. When they did better, they received a bonus proportionate to the amount by which output actually exceeded that benchmark. That made it possible for a group to earn a bonus equal to 100 percent or more of its base wage. Department managers and salaried workers received bonuses based on the plant's return on assets, and all managers above them received bonuses tied to return on shareholder's equity.

Within 10 years, Nucor was able to produce a ton of steel for 40 percent less than its rivals. And by the early 1980s, when the standard output in the steel industry was 10 tons an hour, Nucor workers averaged 30 tons an hour, nearly tripling their base wage.

Minimal Layers

Ken referred to the Nucor incentive system as "Lean and Mean." Lean meant minimal staffing. As a result, the company had few layers of management. In fact, Ken's goal was to invert the typical organizational pyramid. Take a look at Nucor's organizational chart:

Chairman / CEO

Vice President / Plant Manager

Department Manager

Supervisor

Plant Worker

Ken said that the 5th person you talked to at Nucor would always be him. Employees joked that if the janitor got four promotions, he'd have Ken's job. This organizational structure reduced labor costs and paperwork and created a sense that top management was hands-on and in close touch with operations in the field.

The "Mean" side of the incentive system was a tough stand on absences and tardiness. Production employees who arrived for work more than 15 minutes late lost their bonus for the day. If they were more than 30 minutes late, they lost their bonus for the week. That policy caused a high turnover rate among first-year employees, but those who stayed subsequently became big believers in the system and its *esprit de corps*.

Treat People as Equals

Incentive systems aligned managers' and hourly employees' interests, but they were only the start. Senior executives did not enjoy traditional perks like company cars, corporate jets, executive dining rooms, or reserved parking places. Instead, they flew coach and ate lunch in Nucor's version of an executive dining room (a local deli). Workers and management had the same holidays, vacation schedules, and insurance programs.

One of Ken's attempts at creating equality among workers failed. It was tradition in the steel industry that supervisors and managers wore different color hardhats than production workers. Ken was never comfortable with this colorized class system, so he decided that at Nucor, everyone would wear green ones. The push-back was phenomenal, and ultimately he had to back off. It turned out that in an emergency, maintenance people had to be quickly identified, so they were allowed to wear yellow hats, and all visitors would wear white hats. Ken took a whipping, but he showed how serious he was about leveling the playing field at Nucor.

Instead of manipulating workers — which Ken considered a company destroyer — he built a culture that motivated them. With this in mind, the Iverson Credo was born:

1. Everyone must know what is expected and goals should not be set too low.

2. Everyone must understand the rewards, which should be objective and clearly delineated.

3. Everyone must know where to go to get help. The company must have a system that makes it clear to employees who to talk to when they're confused or upset.

4. Employees must have a real say. They should participate in defining goals, determining working conditions, and establishing production processes.

5. Management must provide a feedback system so that employees always know how they, their group, and the company are doing at all times.

Motivating teams of workers had a number of unintended effects. At one Nucor plant, workers would linger around the parking lot after their shifts, waiting until supervisors went home before sneaking back in and helping the next shift.

Encourage Innovation

At Nucor, Ken created a culture that encouraged innovation. He believed that innovation should emanate from the minds of employees motivated and empowered to make decisions. Workers were urged to try new methods, learn from their failed efforts, and then try again. It was understood that everyone would benefit from the group's successes.

Indeed, Ken was fond of saying that strange ideas about improving the company were vitally important to Nucor's success. He figured Nucor could be dramatically successful if he was right only 51 percent of the time. The result was a risk-taking culture where a handful of unorthodox initiatives were always swirling around. Ultimately, it was some of these hare-brained notions separated Nucor from the competition.

Without a formal R&D department or corporate engineering group, Nucor seemed an unlikely industry leader in technology. But lightning struck when it adopted the "mini-mill" concept, first developed in Europe and Japan, at its plant in Darlington, South Carolina. Unlike integrated steel companies, mini-mills did not start with iron ore; rather, they converted scrap steel into finished steel using small-scale electric furnaces. Once Nucor got its collective mind around the technology, it became the low-cost producer in the industry.

But mini-mills had a downside: Until the mid-1980s they could not produce the flat steel products required by certain high-end customers. Lightning struck again when Nucor gambled on a thin-slab casting technology developed by a German firm. Engineers from more than 100 companies had visited the founder, but the technology was unproven on a large scale, and only

Nucor adopted it. The new plant cost several hundred million dollars to build, approximately five times that year's net earnings. But since the technology was scalable, Nucor soon moved into higher-margin products – once again as the low-cost producer.

Culture

Nucor's success did not rest on proprietary technology. Its main innovations were available to all steel companies. While Ken was proud of the Company's technological achievements, he felt its culture of fostering continuous improvements had a bigger impact, accounting for 70 percent of its success. As one competitor noted, Nucor was a throwback to the agrarian idea that if all the farmers worked hard and helped each other, they could collectively survive and meet with success. Stories abounded of production workers who improved operations by instituting small changes. Management was often the last to know.

Marshalling and motivating the intellectual resources of thousands of employees helped Nucor create tremendous shareholder value. From Ken's second year on the job, Nucor never lost money, not even for a single month. Between 1980 and 1990, as the six main integrated producers were reducing their combined steelmaking capacity by nearly half, Nucor doubled in size. By the 1990s, Nucor was generating $1.50 in sales for every dollar in property, plant and equipment it invested to the industry's $0.95. By the time Ken retired, Nucor's market value had grown by more than $1 billion.

Ultimately Ken achieved something that few other managers could: he got workers to identify their own interests fundamentally with those of management. In so doing, he also aligned management's interests with investors. He also forever changed the steel industry. But perhaps his most lasting influence on business was in pioneering the use of culture as a competitive weapon. At Nucor, it turned out, steel was just a by-product of the shining culture.

BLUEPRINT

Nucor Steel is the only public company profiled in this book. But the principles that made it such an extraordinary business under Midas Manager Ken Iverson are applicable to all companies:

1. Align employee, manager, and investor interests by motivating and incentivizing the right behavior. Ken built Nucor's business model on trust and never laid off a single employee. His bonus system ensured that all employees knew where they stood on a weekly basis.

   Under Ken, production workers and managers were on the same page. Each understood that they were all in the same boat and would succeed or fail together. Instead of enforcing their wills, which is typical for managers at large companies, Nucor managers worked for the hourly employees. This was evident when new managers joined the company: the company discouraged them from sending e-mails to workers, giving directives, or offering suggestions unless solicited. Ken told one young manager that "unless an employee asks you a question, he probably isn't interested in what you have to say." At the same time, Nucor expected managers to be available to support workers no matter how trivial the request. This might have required getting a worker a pair of gloves or a tool. Once the manager gained their trust, employees eventually involved her in more meaningful assignments.

   Taking a long-term view of the business was especially challenging for someone in Ken's position. He was the chief executive of a large public company. In typical fashion, he said CEOs had to decide which master they would serve: the speculator who wants a quick return or investors who desire long-term gains. Obviously, he chose the latter.

2. Simplify employee communication. During Ken's tenure, Nucor didn't have a mission statement. He felt they were typically just flowery words that didn't affect the workers. Nucor workers knew the mission because it was constantly discussed with and without management input.

Although his general managers ran the business, Ken knew delegation without information was suicide. At the same time, too much information was as bad as too little information. So he used a one-page flash report to manage the company. Ken believed that the critical success factors for nearly any business could be summarized on a single page.

Communicating with employees often occurred in "town meetings." In these, every employee had the opportunity to speak his or her mind. If employees felt they were not being heard, they were encouraged to call Ken directly. He got a couple dozen such calls each year. Most CEOs would consider this obtrusive, but Ken considered them opportunities to connect with the shop floor.

3. Create an environment where mistakes are tolerated. Pushing decision-making down to the lowest level might have been the most important Iverson imprint on Nucor. He believed the company was better off tapping the intellectual resources housed in its employees than funding a big R&D staff. By fostering an atmosphere of risk-taking without reprisal, employees took ownership of their decisions.

Under Ken, Nucor relied heavily on trial and error in making decisions. Ken claimed that each Nucor facility had literally tons of equipment hidden away that didn't quite work as hoped. It's not that he wanted to foster failure; rather, his culture empowered employees to innovate.

4. Key managers walked the walk. Nucor's offices were known for their Spartan furnishings. There were no special perks for managers. In fact, when Ken was CEO, he answered his own phone. If the company suffered a down year, it hit everyone's pocketbook. One such year saw him take a pay cut to just over $100,000 even though the average CEO salary was five or six times that. Ken said he would have been ashamed to get a big paycheck when Nucor employees had taken such a hit.

5. Align stakeholder interests. Good businesses work well for all involved. Simple as that.

A Midas company, Nucor Steel is the rare public firm that can be a role model for privately held businesses. Take the last point. Aligning stakeholder interests is one of the most important activities for managers of any kind of company, but especially if the manager is also the owner. What's amazing is that so few of them succeed. Many owners drain their private companies of important resources to satisfy their personal needs and then wonder why they can't grow the business. Ken Iverson met this challenge years ago, leaving a legacy for all to see.

26

New Rules Revisited

On September 11, 2001, the United States was thrust into a global war with terrorists. At about the same time, China entered the World Trade Organization. The combination of these events birthed the Conceptual Age and thrust U.S. businesses into a global war of their own.

Both actions — one political, one economic — trace their roots to Internet-enabled globalization and a changing of the rules. There have been a number of business Ages in history, each with its own rules for creating business wealth. With every new Age, the ability to adapt to these new rules has divided winners from losers. Adaptation is rarely easy. Until the Information Age, it took a generation for companies to re-formulate their business models. This is because people formed the backbone of change and people could change only incrementally. With the dawning of the Information Age, technology became the spine of change, for the first time enabling exponential change.

But the Conceptual Age requires more than just transformation. It also demands holistic, multi-dimensional thinking. Business owners must conceive and plan their way to success. Operational excellence is no longer enough, as it was during the efficiency-minded Information Age. In the Conceptual Age, that is merely the starting point.

My dad, a business owner who is the model of self-reliance, once told me that the only security any of us had was what was between our ears. That certainly describes life in the Conceptual Age. Today, the most important skills center on the human mind, or more precisely, on the two hemispheres of our brains. The Information Age worked the left side; the current Age works both the left and right sides. In other words, the left-brain capabilities that powered the Information Age, while still necessary in the Conceptual Age, are no longer sufficient for success.

The skill sets Americans need now are based on right-brain functions like understanding design and creating markets. In a world where most resources are available to everyone, the creativity to conceive of doing more with less separates winners from losers. Finally, artsy people will inherit the earth!

Let's again consider the new rules of wealth creation.

1. Every person working in or for a business must create value to remain employed.

2. Job security is a function of the number of value-creating skill sets a person possesses.

3. A company can expand its returns through arbitrage if its managers understand how to exploit market opportunities.

4. Companies should adopt conceptual business models to create wealth. As such, a company should control – not own – its process chain.

5. In order to make good investment and financing decisions, and thereby create wealth, managers must raise their Private Finance I.Q.

In the Conceptual Age, every person working in or for a business must create value to remain employed. Learning multiple skill sets that all create value is everyone's personal responsibility. It is no longer a company's or government's responsibility to ensure this.

A company can expand its returns via arbitrage if its managers understand how to exploit market opportunities. Arbitrage strategies create returns that are greater than the underlying risk, but they depend on designing solutions that are broadly conceived. For instance, implementing the "buy left, sell right" strategy in Chapter 10 requires a manager to study and understand market segmentation. Likewise, implementing an arbitrage strategy that enables the company to be viewed in a more favorable market segment requires thinking outside the context of the firm. Properly executed, arbitrage strategies can generate amazing returns. They should be employed whenever possible.

Companies should adopt conceptual business models to create wealth. A conceptual business model enables a manager to do more with less. Instead of owning every step in the process chain, companies following conceptual business models leverage outside resources. Command and control is out, collaboration is in, and designing solutions with a high value proposition for the customer is the signature skill of this Age.

Conceptual models also exploit what globalization gives us: niche opportunities. In another paradox of this Age, as global markets get bigger, individual opportunities get smaller. Successful private companies are increasingly just amalgams of niches. And since technology is now the backbone of change, instant niched companies are now possible, too. In prior Ages, it took decades to build substantial wealth, but by following the new rules, Midas Managers are doing it in just a few years.

In order to make wealth-creating investment and financing decisions, managers must raise their Private Finance IQs. Most managers earn their stripes in operations or marketing while finance is left to someone else. This needs to change. One can only make use of private finance strategies when one understands value worlds, cost of capital, and business transfers. For example, a key decision every manager faces is whether to make an investment in the business. Private finance provides a framework to make sure those decisions are adding value.

What else has changed? Consider what the new rules have wrought:

- Intellectual capital, not financial capital, is king
- Giving up ownership is generating greater productivity
- Hoarding of best practices and proprietary ideas has given way to sharing, collaboration, and open-source movements
- Instead of owning every step of the process chain, businesses are outsourcing the ones that don't add value
- Innovation is trumping economies of scale

The Conceptual Age is a time of paradoxes. Perhaps none is greater than the call to abandon all rules. It certainly is a confusing time. The past is no longer predictive, so what a manager knows to be true because it has worked before is now open to question. For instance, what really bankrupted the major airlines, high energy costs, or the inability of its managers to come up with more effective business models? It's like executives at American, United and US Airways, as well as many other American business leaders, decided that the steadfast captain of the Titanic had it right and the iceberg was the one that was wrong. But success today is reserved for those who can reconceptualize themselves and their business models to win the game.

How to Play the Game

Business is a game, albeit one with serious consequences. Like poker, winners in business both understand the rules and can predict and exploit behavior of players better than their opponents. This is what makes periods of change such a dangerous time for us all.

Imagine if all of the rules of baseball were changed one day without warning. Instead of a glove, players had to catch the ball with buckets strapped to their heads. Bats were taped to legs, and pitchers delivered the ball from behind their backs. A lot of major league players would be out of work.

Such is the case in the Conceptual Age. The rules have changed. The players that have adapted to the changing rules of business are starting to dominate. And you think it's competitive now. In a few years, every space in business will be taken over by companies that have adopted conceptual business models and are leveraging their strengths to add value. Those that haven't will be out of the game.

Playing the game means getting strategic. Most owners are forever stuck in tactics, also known as day-to-day operations. An owner of a trucking company with 100 vehicles typically spends more time keeping gas tanks full than thinking about business models. It's human nature to rely on what we know, and we know how to think in discrete elements. Think about how most of us have been educated: First period they terrorize us with our own language; second period is math, because our attention spans fade after lunch; third period is history, and so on. At what point do we ever learn to think holistically or strategically? For most managers, never. Little wonder we're having a tough time coping with the new rules.

The Strategy Thing - Revisited

My favorite definition of strategy comes from chess. It goes like this: Tactics is knowing what to do when there is something to do; strategy is knowing what to do when there is nothing to do. But experience does matter: Midas Mentors say appropriate strategies always present themselves. Perhaps some basic comparisons between tactical and strategic thinking will help make this clearer:

Thinking

Tactical	Strategic
Sergeant	General
Player	Coach
Operations	Business model
Sales	Marketing

Generals devise strategies to win the war, while sergeants apply tactics in the field to win the battle. Operations involve daily activities, while business models involve strategic positioning. A coach designs a game plan, and the players execute it. And marketing sets the condition for sales.

This last comparison is especially poignant. Companies that employ a "Vice President of Sales and Marketing" don't get it. Marketing is a strategic function and, at the least, should be stated first. Frankly, the same person can't effectively work in both roles. The job should be split into more useful titles, such as: "Vice President of Making Markets" and "Vice President of Closing Deals." At least these titles respect the differences in the two functions.

How do you get strategic? This requires a behavioral change that is beyond the reach of many business owners and managers. Either they can't do it, or they won't. In either event, they will forever be tactical thinkers, and eventually, these tacticians will be overtaken by more strategic competitors. Lifestyle-driven business owners, those who choose a paycheck over a payload, those who are not creating value via their businesses, are poised for a dramatic change in lifestyles alright, and not for the better.

But Midas Managers give us hope. We don't have to devise a wealth-creating strategy of our own; we can simply apply one of theirs. By following their examples, we can mitigate considerable risk since it's almost always easier and more productive to copy someone else's successful business practices than to create your own. This is what keeps authors of self-help books in high cotton. But strategic thinking is not as linear as many of the stories in this book might indicate. They've been told in discrete elements because that is how we've been taught to learn. In real life, owners need to bundle strategies together or simultaneously pursue several of them if they want to meet their financial goals.

The main constraint now is our imagination. Today, we all bear personal responsibility for re-thinking our behavior to help us compete in the Conceptual Age. This will be difficult. It requires us to think strategically. It requires us to scale an unending series of walls. It's a chess match on steroids. It's a high-stakes poker game. It's a game we must win if we want to continue to succeed in business.

NOTES

NOTES

NOTES

NOTES

NOTES

NOTES

NOTES

NOTES

NOTES